TEACHING
OLD-FASHIONED
VALUES
TO NEW-FASHIONED
KIDS

TEACHING OLD-FASHIONED VALUES TO NEW-FASHIONED KIDS

Josephine Cunnington Edwards

REVIEW AND HERALD® PUBLISHING ASSOCIATION
HAGERSTOWN, MD 21740

This book was
Edited by Susan Harvey
Designed by Bill Kirstein
Cover art by Byron Steele
Typeset: 10.7/11.7 Palatino

PRINTED IN U.S.A.

98 97 96 95 94 93   10 9 8 7 6 5 4 3 2 1

R&H Cataloging Service
Edwards, Josephine Cunnington.
    Teaching old-fashioned values to new-fashioned kids.

    Selections from *Children can be taught* and *In your steps*.

    1. Character education—children. I. Title.
            136.7

ISBN 0-8280-0655-5

DEDICATION

In memory of
my loving husband
who was ever a source of help
and encouragement to me.

Contents

Meet Josephine Cunnington Edwards

Josephine Cunnington Edwards was born on August 24, 1904, in Muncie, Indiana, the tenth child in a family of eleven. Her parents were Seventh-day Adventists, having joined the church not many years before her birth. Her father, David Cunnington, owned a grocery store on the corner of 5th and Vine streets in Muncie. A sign in the front window of the store read "This grocery will be closed every Friday evening before sunset and will not be opened again until after sunset on Saturday evening for the following reasons—" The rest of the space on the sign was taken up by the entire fourth commandment.

Josephine grew up in a busy, bustling household in Muncie and attended the little Adventist church school there. After 8th grade, she went to Indiana Academy, and it was there that she met Lowell Adelbert Edwards. In the spring of 1923, when Josephine was 19, they were married. After the wedding, they took off for Florida in a Model T Ford, where they both taught church school in St. Petersburg. A year later, they returned to Indiana, where Lowell went to work in a factory in Kokomo, his home town. For the next seven years, he worked in various industrial plants in Kokomo and Muncie.

Lowell and Josephine's first son, Robert Elden, was born in Kokomo in 1924, and their second son, Charles Garland, arrived after they had moved to Muncie, in 1926.

In late 1929 the young couple, with their two small boys, moved to Broadview College, just a few miles outside of Chicago, so that Lowell and Josephine could go back to school. They spent four years there, and when Broadview was changed from a senior to a junior college, they moved to Emmanuel Missionary College (now Andrews University), where they both attended school for the next three years.

The Great Depression was in full swing during the seven years Josephine and Lowell struggled to get their college education. There were no outside funds coming in, and no government loans or other assistance. All the money for tuition and living expenses had to come from whatever the young couple could earn during the hours when they weren't attending classes. Drawing on his previous experience in industry, Lowell worked as a foreman in the paint department at both colleges. Josephine also helped out with the finances, sometimes by baking homemade bread. Even the boys got into the act by weeding carrots and picking tomatoes during the summer months.

A teaching job turned up for Josephine during the school year of 1936-37. Leaving Lowell behind to finish his training at EMC, she moved back to Kokomo with the two boys, where for $15.00 a month and free room and board, she taught all eight grades in the little church school. The following year, she taught at a small school in Glenwood, Michigan, close enough to the college for the young family to be together almost every weekend. By this time, Josephine had already launched her writing career, and had purchased a 1926 Chevrolet for the grand sum of $25, earned with the fees she occasionally received for her articles and stories.

After seven years of struggle, Lowell graduated from college in the spring of 1938 (the same year Josephine published her first book). The faithful old 1926 Chevy took them to their new teaching post in Minneapolis, even though by this time, the car had deteriorated to the point where the doors on the passenger side had to be tied shut with a rope. Lowell taught the ninth and tenth grades at Minneapolis Junior Academy, and Josephine the seventh and eighth. Together, their salaries totaled $125 a month. In the years that followed, they taught at Maplewood Academy near Hutchinson, Minnesota, and then at Oak Park Academy in Nevada, Iowa.

In 1945, the Edwards family was called to mission service in Africa. Eager to serve the Lord wherever He wanted them, they moved to Nyassaland, now known as Malawi. While there, they adopted a black African student, Alice Princess Msumba.

They returned to the United States in 1952 and accepted teaching assignments at Broadview Academy, the scene of their first college days 20 years before. Then in 1954 they joined the staff of Faith for Today in New York, where Josephine was involved in scriptwriting for the TV program. In the late 50s, they moved to Ellijay, Georgia, where Josephine taught school and Lowell was the pastor of the Seventh-day Adventist church.

Lowell died in 1962. After his death, Josephine accepted a call to teach at Oakwood College in Huntsville, Alabama. This college for Black Christian youth held a special attraction for her, since her adopted daughter, Alice Princess, and her husband were attending college there. They had come to the United States for their education as a result of a letter Josephine had written to the *This Is Your Life* television show. The show had paid the expenses for the young people to come to the U.S.

Josephine found herself restless and unsettled after her husband's death. She left Oakwood for a teaching position at Gem State Academy in Caldwell, Idaho, followed by several other teaching jobs in various parts of the country. Her last teaching assignment was at a church school in Antioch, California, where two of her grandsons, James Lowell and James Joseph, were practicing medicine. This gave her an opportunity to teach some of her own great-grandchildren!

Josephine and Lowell's oldest son, Bob, grew up to be a much-loved singer of gospel music. For 24 years he was a member of the King's Heralds Quartet, and also worked as a producer of the daily *Voice of Prophecy* broadcast.

His younger brother, Charlie, has been a pastor in the Indiana, Kentucky-Tennessee, and New England Conferences of Seventh-day Adventists, and a youth director in Upper Columbia and Northern California. He retired in

1990. Together, Bob and Charlie have presented their parents with 7 grandchildren and 15 great-grandchildren.

Alice Princess Msumba presently teaches psychology at a university in San Diego.

Today Josephine lives in Milton Freewater, Oregon. Although she has been officially retired for many years, and at the time of this writing is 87 years old, she continues a back-breaking schedule of appointments not only in North America, but overseas as well. She is beloved all over the world as a master of the art of storytelling, and is known to millions through her many books.

Foreword

"He has evened the path to life, even for children. And parents are required in His name to lead them along the narrow path. God has appointed us a path suited to the strength and capacity of children."—*The Adventist Home,* p. 281.

W*ithout loss of temper,
but decidedly, parents are to say
to their children, No, and
mean it.''*

—*Child Guidance,* p. 101.

CHAPTER 1

Children Can Be Taught to Obey

"Don't forget, Mama, he's trained."

The whole universe of God moves smoothly by the precision of obedience to inviolable laws. God is no friend of undisciplined living. "If ye love me, keep my commandments," says He. "For this is the love of God, that we keep his commandments: and his commandments are not grievous." "He that saith, I know him, and keepeth not his commandments, is a liar, and the truth is not in him." Strong words, but true.

Obedience is the most logical thing in the world. The deeper we go into physical science and history, into botany, zoology, mathematics, and astronomy, the more we see the value of obedience to the laws of the Creator.

Just as surely as all scientific advances depend upon obedience to certain fixed laws, so is a beautiful and holy character and a joyful life dependent upon obedience. We cannot ignore this fact any more than we can ignore the law of gravity by walking confidently out of a fortieth-story window. The ground will be there to meet us, just as surely as night follows day. People know and recognize gravity to be a law to be reckoned with, and no amount of philosophizing on their part will change it one iota. A king or a beggar, a thief or a theologian, will fall with equal rapidity, and the result will be the same.

Our Saviour came to die because of man's disobedience to law which had separated the human race from their Heavenly Father. He obeyed the will of the Father as He wants us to do. He said, "Not my will, but thine, be done." And the disciples who learned to love Him in His brief ministry joyfully yielded up their lives rather than go contrary to His will. If the gospel of obedience was glorious in the days of Christ, is it not even more so in these latter days, so filled with wickedness and lawlessness? Our love for Christ and our gratitude for the gift of salvation creates in us the desire to obey His will.

Many problems of youth today stem from lack of training. A mother and her child were watching a monkey perform tricks in a show. Presently the mother remarked to her child, "Oh, Jennie, I wish you would mind as well as that monkey does!"

The child looked at her mother knowingly. "Don't forget, Mama, he's trained," she informed her mother with more wisdom than she realized.

Even babies can learn what No means, and once said, it should always mean just that. There should be no exceptions. I have heard parents say No thunderously and then, with no further word, allow the child to do what he or she has been forbidden. All of us have known children who studiously ignore everything they are told to do because they are clever enough to know none of the threats will be enforced.

Many children are reared on thunder and lightning. Nothing grows on that. The story is told of a man who had lived in a lighthouse for 28 years. Every three minutes a whistle blew to warn vessels of danger. The lighthouse keeper grew so used to the sound that he did not hear the whistle at all. He could sleep through the night without noticing it. One night, at one of the intervals, a short circuit in the wiring kept the whistle from blowing. Instantly he awoke from a sound sleep. "What was that?" he cried. Children who are bone-weary of shouts and commands might better be awakened to obedience by a little carefully timed silence.

I once read a book on animal training that had some solid advice that could be transferred to the training of little ones. My children and I tried several of the rules on our little terrier, and he quickly learned many amusing and clever tricks. The book said, "Reward and praise obedience, and punish disobedience every time. Never make an exception. Let him realize that disobedience is always associated with discomfort and disfavor; and that obedience will bring praise and comfort and pleasantness. Use the same words for the same requirement every time. Do not confuse him. He has his limitations. Do not punish him a long time after an offense. He cannot remember what he is being punished for. The time to punish is at the time of the disobedience, and he will associate the unpleasantness with the misdemeanor."

There could not be sounder advice on training. When we taught our puppy to sit up, we said, "Sit up," every time, until he knew what we meant when we said those two words. If he was disobedient or sulky, I gently used the fly swatter. It was not long before he would far rather sit up than be swatted. Moreover, he willingly sat up when he was happy, because the act was always associated with praise, petting, peanuts, or peppermint drops. It was fun for that puppy to obey.

A baby was told not to play with a porcelain vase on a low coffee table. He well knew the meaning of NO. He reached out his tiny hand for the pretty vase. His mother said No, so he withdrew it. The temptation was great, and he soon returned and reached out a small hand again. This time when the mother said No, she spatted the tiny offending hand smartly. He cried for a little while, but went away and played happily for a long time. After about an hour he returned and reached again, his eyes fixed speculatively on his mother's face. He was clever enough to watch narrowly for danger signals. With this, she smacked the baby fingers several times, saying No at every whack. Of course he cried, but he was not really injured. And it is certain that he quite understood that she meant business; No meant just that. He did not bother the vase again—

indeed, he hardly appeared to notice it. But the important thing about the whole thing is this: He knew precisely why his hands were spanked, for they were spanked at the height of the offense, when it was fresh in his mind. In his baby way, the vase was "marked off his list" of acquirable things, for too much trouble was involved in getting possession of it. Every time he had tried to touch it, he had experienced inconvenience. If the mother had not punished him every time, the habit would have taken infinitely longer to break.

Before my little boy could walk he became increasingly curious about a wall plug in our living room. There was a short circuit in it somewhere, and we could not use it. We blew fuses every time we plugged into it. My husband intended to fix it as soon as he could find time. (Nowadays I would have covered it with a plug cover, but I didn't know about those then.) I knew the baby would be shocked if he touched it, and I tried to keep him away by telling him No every time he make a pass in that direction.

One day he was playing near it, and I said No again. He knew what I meant, but he would often try me, even though he knew he would be punished. I was called out of the room for a minute, and while I was attending to some other duty I heard the baby scream. I knew immediately what had happened. He had stuck his finger into the wall plug. I ran to him. Sure enough, there he was, lying on the floor, screaming loudly, and waving his little finger in the air.

I picked him up, sat down in a chair with him, and soothed him as well as I could. Rocking him back and forth, I said, "No, no; baby must not touch. It will hurt baby. Poor baby. It will hurt baby." Presently he stopped crying, slid down from my lap, and sat looking balefully toward the offending plug.

"No, no," he shouted at the plug. I knew then that he understood. The lesson was a hard one, but he developed such a repugnance toward that wall plug that he seldom crossed the room without making a wide arc to avoid going near it.

One of the first lessons a child needs to learn is that he must obey. He must be taught this habit before he is old enough to reason. When this is done gently and persistently, the conflicts that frequently arise in later years between parents and children, or teachers and pupils, will be avoided.

When children are small, it may be necessary to spank them occasionally. This must be done in love, and never overdone. If it can be avoided, and the child is not cheated of the lesson that needs to be learned, it should be avoided.

My baby got a spanking the first time he turned on the gas in my kitchen range. I did not do it for revenge, nor because I was angry, but because there were four lives in danger if I allowed this habit to go unchecked. Reason had not yet entered Baby's young head to a marked degree, and he had to be taught immediately in a way he could understand and remember. Spankings need not be administered often, especially after the children have learned that No means just that.

We all have to meet perverseness in our children and, occasionally, a stubbornness that is hard to master. I have seen young children—indeed, mere babies—hold their breath until they became unconscious if their imperious wills were crossed in the slightest degree. For the child's good, this must not be allowed to go on. But in dealing with these little ones, we must never forget our own childhood. There is not one of us who was not, to some degree, stubborn and obdurate and in need of discipline when he or she was a child.

I once knew some young parents who were of the "broken-record" type with their young son. It was "No, no" and "Don't, don't" all the time, with the child studiously ignoring everything the parents said. Anything the little boy could get his hands on was his until someone took it away from him. Rather than teaching him that he must leave certain things alone, temptation was always removed from him until he came to believe that anything in reach was his by right of discovery. This is a bad attitude for individuals and nations. Wars have been fought over such things.

That is why such an attitude should be rooted out of our children's lives early. (On the other hand, there should not be so many temptations that parents must always say No.) There will never be a time when children (or adults) can have everything they lay their hands on. This child was never taught that some things were for him and some things were not for him at all—and those he must not touch or bother.

In the kitchen his mother patiently removed his eager fingers from the mixer, the stove, and the blender. She was constantly saying, "Don't, precious," or "Stop, baby." But since he did not know from experience that he would be inconvenienced or hurt if he persisted after he had been told not to do a thing, he went merrily on until he was locked out of the room or given some other thing to do that diverted him. His parents had to stand guard all the time, for real danger was involved. Their protests were just so much air to the child. Not only was he learning the wrong lesson about life, but he was constantly in danger of doing serious injury to himself.

Discipline should be a private matter. Parents make a grave mistake when they make every wrong deed public. Mothers will shout, "You just wait until your father comes home and hears of this!" Then the whole day is ruined for the little one. He or she dreads daddy's homecoming, for humiliation is sure to follow, and small errors will be gone over with a fine-toothed comb. This should not be! Little ones should wait with joy and eager anticipation for their working parents to come home. And they, soul weary from their combat with the workday world, want to come home to serenity and happiness. This is no time to sit in judgment, no time to arm for war. Children need a lot of loving every minute. Love is the balm that heals the wounds of the world.

Humiliation never heals or cures, but makes an ugly wound that mortifies and grows malignant. Remember that those who most try our patience most need our love. We cannot follow the timeworn axiom of "treating them as they deserve.'' Had Christ done that, we would all be miserable. ''He was treated as we deserve that we might be treated as He deserves.''

Some parents seem to think it unnecessary to praise children for anything they have done. One parent who disapproved of commendatory words informed me soberly, ''My children have to be good for nothing. Why should I pay them or praise them for being good?''

The Father praised Jesus. ''This is my beloved Son, in whom I am well pleased,'' He said. He was so proud of Job that He spoke thus of him to Satan: ''Hast thou considered my servant Job, that there is none like him in the earth, a perfect and an upright man, one that feareth God, and escheweth evil?''

Nor does God ask us to be good for nothing. The Bible is full of rich promises to the overcomer. ''Eye hath not seen, nor ear heard, neither have entered into the heart of man, the things which God hath prepared for them that love him.'' And, ''Blessed are they that do his commandments, that they may have right to the tree of life, and may enter in through the gates into the city.''

This is not to say that children should be hired to do everything. Very soon they would get such an inflated idea of their own importance that they would refuse to do anything unless a reward were offered. But occasionally, in a variety of ways, gratitude can be expressed to encourage the child.

''I bought some fresh blueberries today, Jennifer, because you like them. You were so patient and kind when the baby was sick last week, and you have done your work so nicely lately. I love to do things you like. It is fun for us all to be happy.''

I told a little boy in one of the schools where I taught that I liked the way he swept the floor. He went out of his way to do perfect work after that and even took my desk into his care. He was always straightening my books and polishing the desk top. He needed the praise and responded positively to it. We cannot expect loyal obedience if we are not friends with our children. That friendship means that obedience will continue even when the loving guide is not watching.

One of the greatest requisites in discipline is that the punishment fit the offense. Some people have resorted to a mode of discipline that we might call saturation—they make the child repeat the offense over and over again. But this I cannot agree with, for it denies the principle behind discipline. Discipline is meant to arrest the wrongdoing and to turn the child about to face the right way. It is to build up the child's convictions against a wrong thing and increase self-control to resist temptation when it recurs.

"Saturation" must be wrong, for if the thing was wrong to do in the first place, why make the child do it again and again, with the idea that he or she will get tired of it? Many parents, and even teachers, think the child will get so bone-weary of the thing that there will be no desire to repeat it. Really now, if it is wrong for the child to stamp and kick and scream, is it good psychology to force him or her to continue it for a protracted time? What reaction will this create in the child's own thinking? Not that what he or she has done is wrong, certainly, but that it irritates you and inconveniences you, and you want him or her to get tired of doing it so that you will not be troubled again soon. This is bad.

If a child clatters down the stairs in heavy shoes, it certainly is neither wise nor good to make him or her repeat this offense several more times for a "lesson." Moreover, there may be other members of the household whose serenity will be banished by the unnecessary noise. It is not good to inflict matters of discipline upon everyone living in the house. The dignified thing is to have discipline as private as possible. No child likes to have his misdeeds published. Parents must not destroy every vestige of their children's pride and self-respect. If a child feels a sense of constant disgrace, he or she may throw discretion to the winds and do all kinds of outrageous things.

Discipline must be "sold" to the child. He or she must realize that you are right, but that there is no insuperable gulf between you. Reconciliation to the right and good way of conduct can never be achieved if there is a disgraceful clash of wills, undignified shouting, and discouraging heckling and nagging. The child will become so discouraged that he or she will think there is no use to try anymore.

It is often the case that one of the parents is unduly harsh and dictatorial with the children and rules them with a rod of iron. They obey the mandates with fear rather than love. The children then get the impression that they must submit to this particular parent because it is his or her arbitrary will. Whether it is right or wrong does not enter into the question. They, the children, are weak; the parent is strong. Right here, boys and girls of spirit and ambition often determine secretly to get away from the galling yoke of bondage. At the earliest opportunity, these children run away from home.

With this sternness, this harshness, another evil looms up. The uncompromising and exacting discipline of one parent may lead the other to be increasingly lax. The children need someone to love and pity them. Their hearts reach out like tender plants toward the warmth and sunshine of understanding and pitying love. The more nurturing parent can do nothing but pour oil on needless wounds. Such a situation is unhappy in the extreme, for the unity of the house is broken, and a house divided against itself cannot stand.

Usually, when restraint is removed, children from a home in which there has been harsh, uncompromising discipline go wild.

Your discipline should inspire love and confidence rather than fear; it should impress indelibly on the tender mind of your children that it is more comfortable and happy to do right; that you, the parent, stand for that right, and that your loving hands are ready to lead your children to happiness and to shield them from things that will blight and ruin their lives. If you can do this, with one hand in the hand of Christ and the other hand grasping the trusting hand of your child, the battle is won.

Dear God,

I'm sure You know about the grief
  Of grubby little boys,
Of certain little dreams denied—
  Desires for better toys;
Having to come in from their play
  To work or sleep or eat.
When mother washes ears, it hurts;
  And candy is so sweet.

I'm sure You understand, dear Lord,
  How much it pains my heart
To see his lips a trembling,
  And see the teardrops start.
When I must make him know to mind
  His daddy's least command—
That he must heed when spoken to,
  I know You understand.

Ah, Father, does it hurt You, too,
  To see me weep and sigh?
To see me writhe at discipline,
  And wring my hands and cry?
Do You recoil from hurting me?
  But, oh, I know You must.
You truly know Your child is frail,
  And made of earthly dust.

So You must get me ready, Lord,
  So I'll be strong to stand.
And I must make my boy obey—
  Yes, Lord, You understand.

To train the young to become
true soldiers of the Lord Jesus
Christ is the most noble work
ever given to man."

—Counsels to Parents and Teachers, p. 166

CHAPTER 2

Children Can Be Taught to Enjoy Working

"Fetch me that bowl of apples, Ike."

Children should be taught to work, for habits of industry have to be woven into the very fabric of life. Opinions are molded in the home. If your front yard is neatly mowed and well cared for, your children are bound to notice if a neighbor's yard is filled with weeds and trash. At school, if your child is neat and clean, he or she will come home and say something like, "Mom, Jason always has buttons off his shirt!" or, "Dad, Brenda never has any tissues, and she just lets her nose run." Children will quickly learn what is nice and what is not if they are taught, and they will soon grow to love to do things that contribute to the comfort of those they love.

But when I speak of children working, I do not mean that their happiness must be diminished by long hours of exacting toil. When I was a child, we lived near a family the father of which "enjoyed" ill health. He was always pursued by some hypochondriacal ailment, while his wife and children worked and struggled to keep body and soul together. Special things were demanded and gotten by the fat "invalid." A large piece of pie lay next to his plate. He ate only butter, but the children and mother had no spread at all. A small carton of cream was bought especially for him every day. One day one of the little girls shyly pointed to a tiny bit of pie that had fallen from the plate.

"Can I have that, Daddy?" she asked.

He seized it and thrust it into his own immense mouth. "No. Daddy's sick."

The children weeded and worked in the vegetable garden all morning; in the afternoon they were sent out to sell the vegetables door to door.

Many a time they leaned against the picket fence surrounding our yard and wistfully watched my brothers and me happily playing a game of croquet. Their faces would light up, showing vicarious joy over some comical antic on our part; then a shade of indescribable sadness would pass over them.

With a sigh, the children would pull themselves away and go on from house to house, selling beets and carrots and green onions. There was no play at nighttime for them, either. It was, "Get off to bed, you. We've all got to get up at 5:00 and set out more onions."

Children should learn to work, but God forbid that it should be as it was in that family! Their cases smacked too much of the horrible practices of the Industrial Revolution in the seventeenth and eighteenth centuries. Children worked 12 to 15 hours a day in the great textile mills and in the mines. Poor mites would creep under the great loom, tying broken threads hour after hour with small fingers that had never learned how to play. Boys were sent down into coal mines to work seven days a week. For years on end they would never see the light of day.

Today there are child labor laws that keep children out of mines and factories, thank God! There are school attendance laws that prevent parents from exploiting their children and depriving them of their just and lawful rights.

Children should have time to play. Puppies roll and yelp and turn somersaults. Human babies, too, need to frolic. They need to shrill and shriek and hide and laugh and climb. They need to kick up their heels like calves and colts.

It is instructive. It is as needful as daily bread. And even play, rightly organized and wisely led, will lead to the love of work.

Wise parents will provide small children with child-sized hoes and rakes and let them help with gardening and yard work. A toy iron and ironing board or other miniature household tools and appliances are fun for both girls and boys when parents are attending to household chores.

My mother was clever. When she stirred up corn bread, I got a small bowl and was allowed to make some too. She knew that children like littleness, and the small eggs from our bantam hens were saved for my childish cooking ventures. I had a small rolling pin, a small bread pan, and my own little pie pans. I was baking bread and cooking simple meals when I was 10 years old. It was not drudgery. It was fun.

As I grew older mother and I became partners in the kitchen. I remember the day when she told me that she had discovered that shredded pineapple was delicious with cottage cheese. "Drain it," she counseled, "and then add a bit more cream."

Then I told her that I had found that shredded cabbage and carrots were also delicious in cottage cheese. "But you add mayonnaise instead of cream," I told her. My little-girl play had grown into a great delight.

Later when I came home from college, my mother would often ask, "Do you know any new recipes?" Of course I did, and we would go into the kitchen and joyfully work them out together. No wonder I like cookbooks and collect them as some people collect stamps. My play had metamorphosed into work of the most useful variety.

Sometimes children are spurred by circumstances to great effort. They awaken early to responsibility that they are jealous to relinquish, for they have chosen it and gain much pride and satisfaction from it. When my great-grandmother was left a widow, she had six children and a barely cleared homestead. Pioneer life was never easy, and her children had to help do all the things necessary for actual existence in those days. But with great-grandfather under the sod, those children believed that they could fare far worse than to pitch in and do the work. They had observed that stepfathers were not always good to their children. Those five brothers and one sister were astute enough to cast their young eyes about, and seeing no one whom they would relish in their father's place, they all got busy.

My own grandmother, who had been taught weaving and spinning almost as soon as she could walk, got work in a nearby cloth mill. The boys worked early and late, striving with all their young strength to take the place of their lost father. They chopped wood, pitched hay, forked manure out of the stables, and made brave plans as to how they would put out the crops in the spring. They were doing a good job, and the whole neighborhood watched with interest. Great-grandmother set up her loom in the front room and began to do custom weaving. After all the household and farm chores of the morning were over, she either spun thread or worked at her loom all the long afternoon. People marveled at the young mother's will to keep her family together. Less determined souls would have given up and apprenticed the children out, as was often the custom in those days. But great-grandmother looked neither to the right hand nor to the left, and went her lonely way. Several eligible men would have been glad to be friendly, but she gave them no encouragement. Her heart was still too sore at the loss of her husband.

Along toward spring a notoriously lazy widower, Peleg Wintergreen, began to cast greedy eyes on her rich acres bordered by sparkling little Buck Creek, which never went dry, and on her slim, comely person and the beauty of her apple-cheeked face, and began to drop in unannounced. Gradually his visits became more frequent, but he did not say a word to great-grandmother about his intentions although he did brag to his companions who sat about the stove in the village store, swapping yarns and whittling. Because he did not declare himself, great-grandmother felt at a loss to put a stop to his "casual" visits.

He usually came slouching in without the polite warning

of a knock, to take his place in great-grandfather's tall splint chair by the fireplace. From that vantage point he could spit tobacco in the general direction of the fire with the greatest of ease. Great-grandmother Janie seethed inwardly to see her clean hearth thus sullied. Her husband had not so much as looked at tobacco. Unfailingly polite and unassertive, Janie went right on with her weaving when he came in, but did not even pretend to entertain him. He did not seem to mind. He would sprawl out in great-grandfather's favorite chair, his Adam's apple rhythmically chinning itself as he contentedly "chawed."

One night Peleg was sitting at his ease, surveying the place proprietorially, when he spied a wooden bowl of apples sitting on the dresser next to the fireplace. Looking across at 10-year-old Isaac, who was whittling a spinning top out of a peg of wood, he demanded curtly, "Fetch me that bowl of apples, Ike. I feel like I could eat a couple or three. They shore look good."

Ike and his brother Val had only that day dug them out of the apple hill in cold-storage where they were kept during the winter. Ike remembered digging through the sharp crust of the snow, and how cold his hands had gotten. He thought of how last fall, he and Val had driven the four miles to town and spent their hard-earned money to buy them from old Grandpa Jones, whose new orchard had begun to bear. Now, without even asking if he could have one, Peleg was demanding the work of their young hands. How could Mother tolerate this unsavory specimen? Young Isaac turned his head away, ignoring Peleg's request. "Do you hear, young feller?" Peleg demanded in a high, nasal voice, calculated to be impressive. Isaac bent his whole energy to the rounding out of the maple peg. Then he looked up and met Peleg's eyes fearlessly.

"I won't," he replied quietly.

Janie heard the conversation from her place behind the loom. Usually she deplored impudence and would have punished any of her children severely for talking so rudely. But this case was different. Peleg was so notoriously lazy, and had gotten so obnoxious, that she brushed Ike's insolence aside as a necessary evil. Before this, she could hardly have dismissed Peleg without some awkwardness, for he had not said why he was coming to see her. But this night he left no doubt as to his intentions.

Turning his chair toward the loom, he addressed Janie in a loud voice: "Have you got a strap hangin' around, Janie?" he asked familiarly. "I'm goin' to give this Ike a dressin' down. He might as well learn first as last who's boss around here. I'm not goin' to have him handin' me any sass when I'm puttin' out the spring crops. He needs just the kind of hidin' a man can give him. Fetch me a strap, Janie." My great-grandmother came out from behind the loom, her lips set in a thin line and fire in her eyes.

"You'd better get your hat and get out of here, Peleg," she said, her voice trembling with anger. "Seems to me you are taking a lot for granted. I never asked you to come and sit here spittin' all over my clean hearth. And you're not goin' to touch Ike, neither. He has been the man of the house since his pappy died. As for your puttin' out my crops, I don't know who ever asked you to. I am sure I didn't."

Peleg, dull-witted as he was, swiftly perceived his mistake. He saw his chances of getting a clean, well-cleared, fertile farm, and a pretty, capable wife growing exceedingly slim. He got to his feet and managed a sickly smile.

"Heh, heh," he croaked feebly at Ike. "You and yer mammy took me plumb serious that time. I've always loved to have my little joke. Janie"—he turned toward the young woman who stood facing him with smoldering eyes—"I'll do well by ye. You need a man, and I need a woman. I'll make yer farm pay ye. Don't see why we can't get right into the harness together."

"Yes, you'll make my farm pay," scoffed the usually unassuming Janie in high sarcasm. "Your homestead is the sorriest place in the whole county. My children and I can run this place better than you can run yours. The weeds would have plumb took your whole place last summer if your poor wife hadn't worn herself out doin' a man's and a woman's work both. Everybody says she died from hard work and unkind treatment. Now you want me and my children diggin' and delvin' for you. Well, we won't. I won't have any man comin' in here taking Chalon's place. He was the best—the best—'' Janie could stand it no longer. She burst into a torrent of weeping. In the midst of the flood, Peleg furtively snatched his hat and took his leave, never to return, much to everyone's relief at Janie's house and everyone's amusement in the neighborhood.

Those children never resented the work that fell to their shoulders, but they were swift to sense injustice, even in the offing.

I once read an old-fashioned poem about a boy who complained bitterly about how life had treated him. His chicks became his mother's hens and roosters. His pig became his father's sow. His carefully reared calf became his father's cow. Children have run away from home for less than that.

Many years ago, when I was teaching school in southern Michigan I had occasion to praise two boys for sweeping snow out of the school entrance. They did so without any request from me, and I praised them for it. Considerable whispering went on between them for the rest of recess, and at noon the boys almost swallowed their lunch whole, they were so eager to get out of doors. I knew something was afoot, but decided to allow them to surprise me. Just before time for the bell to ring, one of them came to the door.

''Come and see,'' he said, a big grin lighting up his face. I followed him. He led me into the woodshed. It was in perfect order. The wood was neatly stacked, and the dirt floor had been swept. They stood there looking up into my face, eager, yes, hungry for the appreciation they knew I would have for them. Our children get hungry for appreciation and praise. If they ask us for bread, do we give them a stone? Then why do we sometimes neglect their other needs?

One early summer day, when my young husband was in his last year of college, our oldest boy approached me and began to whisper excitedly into my ear.

"Charlie and I have been talking. You and Daddy are working too hard. We are going down to see if the farm has any work we could do to help pay Daddy's school bill."

I could hardly keep back the tears while I assured him that was a noble and generous thought.

Off they marched down the road, two loving and determined little figures, eager to share our worries.

When the monthly school statements came, nobody was prouder and happier than two little boys.

"Bob . . . labor . . . $6.54"

"Charles . . . labor . . . $5.96"

"Mother," Bob said earnestly, "that adds up to $12.50. Daddy would have to work a long time to get that, wouldn't he?"

We assured them that they had done a wonderful thing. Their hearts were warmed with praise, and we went on a picnic to celebrate our bonanza. They kept up their voluntary work all summer. They weeded, packed tomatoes, and helped to put baskets together. They loved it. It helped, too. We had a gala occasion every time a statement came out. It was not drudgery, for they had chosen to do so; responsibility had awakened in their hearts.

Once I was trying to go to summer school and keep house at the same time. A heavy examination held me until 12:30 one hot August day. I was worried about getting lunch for my husband and sons, and hurried all the way home. There I found that my husband had already gone back to work, fed. Two small boys, responsibility written importantly on their faces, waited.

"We got lunch," they informed me.

"Charlie cut the bread and sliced the tomatoes," Bob said. "He cut his finger, too." Charlie displayed an elaborately bandaged digit.

"I fried the potatoes; Daddy said they tasted good."

I sat down to eat, with the little fellows hovering near, anticipating my every want. It was a minor thing that they had set the black frying pan with the potatoes still hissing in it in the middle of my best lunch cloth. Their hearts were glowing with the joy of their labor, and that was the important thing.

The older I grow, the more I realize that a superabundance of everything is often detrimental to a child's development. Instead of putting responsibility on their children gradually, some surround them from the hour of their birth with every comfort that money can buy. We all know that this does not develop character in children. Many of the great men and women of the world were reared in humble circumstances—indeed often in poverty, where they learned early to think and fend for themselves. But to live in a beautiful home surrounded by luxury without responsibility, to be pampered and coddled, to have too much money to spend and too much leisure time to fritter away—how subtly such "advantages" can put a wrong definition on real life.

Yes, children can be taught to work, and to like it, for work and its rewards are richer and tastier than the fruit of idleness. Jesus taught the dignity of labor by His years in the carpenter shop in Nazareth.

If parents work in patience and love, earnestly endeavoring to help their children to reach the highest standard of purity and modesty, they will succeed.''

—The Adventist Home, p. 208.

CHAPTER 3

Children Can Be Taught Wholesome Attitudes Toward Sex

"Professor Johnson, I do believe you are pregnant."

There seem to be two great mistakes that parents make—mistakes as wide apart as the swing of the pendulum. One is that they evade the subject of sex altogether and never mention it to their children. On the other extreme, some parents tell their children too much, while they are much too young; and they tell them in such a way that they are likely to make extremely embarrassing observations.

One tot was told that auntie was very fat because she was going to have a baby. The child was intrigued, and must have concluded mentally that all fat people were expecting to help populate the earth. The mother said further, "We call anyone who is going to have a baby, 'pregnant.' "

"Auntie is pregnant?" the child asked.

"Yes, dear," replied the mother.

That night a college professor came to call upon the family. Elaine had not yet gone to bed. Presently she came close and looked the dignified gentleman over carefully.

"Professor Johnson, I do believe you are pregnant!" she observed shrilly, looking pointedly at his vast frontage.

Everyone was embarrassed, but the dignified Professor Johnson was so utterly mortified that he beat a hasty retreat.

It is necessary to avoid prudishness and false modesty in teaching our little ones, but we should teach them not to belch or spit or talk about emptying their bladders or bowels in public. Children are not secretive, and they are most impulsive; therefore it is wise to mix a bit of discretion with the sex education we give them. We must remember their years and understanding.

I suppose one of the most ideal places to rear a child is on a farm, where calves, kittens, puppies, and foals are born, and where chicks are hatched. Healthy attitudes about procreation develop naturally. No one goes about snickering and whispering and joking at lambing time. Whole families stay up, concerned and anxious, to take care of the ewes. It is all part of the plan of a just and provident God.

Again, such knowledge should be so gradually imparted as not to create a great astonishment or absorption in the mind of the child.

I would tell my children quite matter-of-factly, "Don't pick up kitty and squeeze her now, for she is going to have kittens. A little later we would notice the cat searching around in closets or under beds. I would say, "Oh, look at kitty! She is hunting a bed to put her kittens in!" Then together we would fix a box with straw or grass or an old coat for the cat. If the children saw the kittens being born, we took this matter of factly. The kitten's mother certainly did and the children did also.

The way a parent answers innocent queries will be the test as to whether the child will come back for more information. If a parent scolds the child for asking about sex, the child will probably never go to the parent again when in need of understanding on the subject. Children are extremely sensitive to the fact of their immaturity. Sex knowledge should come as gradually and as naturally as learning to talk.

Some parents are extremely careless about watching over their children. They will allow them to go for hours, even days, to play with a distant playmate. And because many, many parents are careless, it is a dubious practice to allow a child to spend the night away from home. Conversation among unsupervised children can so often drift to subjects better discussed with mother or father. And in these days when child abuse and diseases such as AIDS are so prevalent even the smallest children need accurate information, matter-of-factly presented by loving parents.

One lad went up to his playmate and whispered, snickering, "There's a crack in our bathroom door. My mom's taking a bath. Come and look."

The little playmate looked up in disgust. "That's silly," he replied. "Who wants to see anyone take a bath? That's nothin'." A bath is no curiosity to the child raised in a healthy family atmosphere.

Yet even in being matter-of-fact lies great danger. Some parents make the grave mistake of allowing their boys and girls to bathe together. A bath should be a private procedure and a dignified necessity. It is extremely wise to teach the child to keep himself to himself. Yet there are some parents who will even share the bathtub with an adolescent. Such parents fondly assure themselves that "our children are different. They do not think a thing about it!" There could not be worse self-deception. Such looseness in ordering the lives of children has led to abuses and subsequent emotional distress that cannot be eradicated in the child's entire lifetime.

The delicate changes that take place in the child's body as he or she approaches puberty make it a natural thing to wonder and search for answers to questions that loom large in the mind. Happy are those parents whose children feel free to come to them with these questions. Sometimes a child will come and ask the meaning of words that almost take the parent's breath away, but not an expression must cross the parent's face that would drive the child away and cause him or her to seek other sources of information.

Then, early must begin an education that will build a love and respect for purity and a loathing and horror of evil practices. To an adolescent one can say, "Oh, look at that woman! God pity her!" (In the event of seeing a prostitute.)

"Why, Mom?"

"She sells her body to any man who pays her a certain sum of money. And, you know, neither she nor the men who abuse her will ever see the pure beauty of heaven unless they repent. That is why God wrote the seventh commandment in the Ten Commandments. He wants people to be pure and good and clean."

It is wise ever to keep in front of the child ideals of purity and truth. I kept a framed picture of Sir Galahad on my living room wall. His motto was, "My strength is as the strength of ten, because my heart is pure." The look on the face of the great knight was an inspiration in itself. He seemed to be looking beyond the petty things of earth to the power and beauty of the Invisible One.

One day some teenagers I know saw a blind baby. The father was known to have been unfaithful to his wife, and even to have sought the company of prostitutes. In answer to their questions, the mother of the child unhesitatingly told them why her baby was blind.

"When a man goes to women who sell themselves and their purity, he sometimes gets terrible diseases that are very hard to cure. Many times the man passes them on to his innocent children. Poor Martha will have to go through life without her eyesight because of her father's wickedness."

"But that is not right, Mom. Martha did not do anything bad. Why should she suffer for her father's sins?"

"Of course it isn't right. But that is the way it is with sin. No sinner can say, 'My folly is my own.' The whole world is full of suffering because sin is not fair or right. The innocent and the good alike are dragged in on the heels of other people's wickedness. There is nothing just or right or good about sin. That is the reason we all want to be rid of it."

Children have a right to know about the real facts of life. They have a right to expect truth and frankness from their natural informants, their parents. But only a fraction get the proper information from father or mothers; they are too busy, too dilatory, or too delicate minded to train the children they have brought into the world.

Parents have to be all eyes and all ears, and need to proceed on their knees to save their children from sin. Every tactful word that can be dropped that will help to mold young minds and young opinions must be prayerfully utilized.

Another great help in keeping the child pure and clean, mentally and morally, is to keep him busy. Not at just work, work, work, but at hobbies, games, tasks, music, art, and books. A garden from which the products can be sold is a wonderful thing for the child. Go with him to the garden and gladden his heart with your happy companionship, with secrets you two alone can share. What must you do that is more important? Then, what could be a better hobby than music or art? Even if he is not especially gifted, you can train him to understand and enjoy them. Without an appreciation of music and art we miss much of the loveliness in this life.

A generation or two ago few parents shared any knowledge of sex with their children. They often left the impression that sex was nasty, that anything connected with reproduction was animalistic and degrading. Much unhappiness and maladjustment have resulted from such attitudes. Nowadays the pendulum has swung to the other extreme, and young people are well-informed, to say the least. Some may question whether outspoken flagrance is an improvement.

But concern about this outspokenness gives no excuse for parents to refrain from telling their children about sex in a happy, beautiful way. Not all at once, of course—there could not be a worse mistake—but a slowly unfolding revelation as the child needs it and is ready for it.

The sunlight of wholesome knowledge can dispel the fogs of morbid curiosity and misinformation. All movements to bring this about are commendable indeed. Parents who do not themselves take this responsibility are sinners against society. The Saviour never put any premium on ignorance.

*E*ncourage in your children a truthful, honest disposition. Let them never have occasion to doubt your sincerity and exact thoughtfulness."

—*Spiritual Gifts*, vol. 2, p. 256.

CHAPTER 4

Children Can Be Taught to Be Honest

"I think I had better be punished for that."

Ayoung mother took her baby girl to town one day in her stroller. The child was a pretty little thing of two, with sunny hair, blue eyes, and a radiant smile. The way was long and the day was hot, but Debbie chattered happily all the way and flashed contagious smiles at every passerby.

The mother finished her shopping as quickly as she could, and started home. When they were almost there, she noticed a red ball in little Debbie's hand.

"Where did you get that ball, Debbie?"

"In the 'tore," replied the little one.

"Oh, then we will have to take it back," replied the mother quickly. "You see, we did not give the woman any money for it. When we do not pay for a thing we take at a store, it is very bad. Jesus called it stealing. We do not want to hurt dear Jesus that way, do we, Debbie?"

Resolutely the mother turned the stroller around. Her feet were tired, and her arms and back ached from pushing the stroller. All the way to town she talked kindly to the child about the wrong of taking things, and how people must never do that. Arriving at the store, she took the child immediately to the toy department.

"Debbie wants to give back a ball she took," the mother

said sweetly. "You see, she did not know that we have to pay money for things we want, so she wants to give it back."

Debbie stood up in her stroller and gave the ball back to the clerk. Tears were streaming down her rose-petal cheeks. Not because her mother had talked harshly to her, because she had not. But because, childlike, she had fancied the bright toy and wanted to keep it.

"I wike dat ball," she sobbed.

"Why don't you buy it for her?" pleaded the clerk.

"Not today," replied the wise young mother. "Another day, yes, but not today. This is my baby's first lesson in restitution. I do not want to spoil it." The walk back to town had been hard. The mother was tired, but she gladly gave of her strength that her little one might learn a valuable lesson. Some mothers would have said, "I will take it back tomorrow," or "I will pay them the thirty-nine cents the next time I go to town." Each of these solutions would have discharged the family debt for the mistake—to everyone but Debbie. She would not have been dealt with honestly. She would have been the one who was cheated. It pays to be honest with our children.

One of the most common errors that mothers and fathers fall into is to shout threats and recriminations at their children that they never intend to carry out. Indeed, they would be jailed if they did. What would happen if children were "skinned alive" or "beaten to a pulp," had their "heads knocked off" or their "necks broken," as parents have many times extravagantly threatened to do? That these horrible things are often shouted in anger is no excuse. Such talk is a form of dishonesty, not to mention child abuse.

Even such extravagant declarations as, "Get that noisy thing out of here; it's driving me crazy," are nothing short of prevarication. It is not driving you crazy. It is annoying you. I know parents who were so easily annoyed that they drove their children out of their very hearts and lives. And try to get them back, once you have driven them away! It is easier to pick up spilled water.

A certain mother had carefully taught her children that

they must not eat between meals. She was gratified to see that they were hungry for every meal, and little inclined to criticize and find fault with what was set before them.

"Oh, no, dear," the mother replied to her child's request for a snack. "It is only an hour till supper time; wait until then, and we will all have some oranges."

The little girl said nothing, but ran off to play.

The mother decided to lie down for a few minutes before she started supper. She had almost dropped off to sleep when she heard soft footfalls in the dining room. Through the double doorway she saw her daughter tiptoe up to the table, reach up, take an orange, and retire as quietly as she had come in.

The mother was saddened at the thought that her little daughter had resorted to dishonesty and deceit to gratify her small desires. She was too wise, however, to arise in wrath and shout at her erring child. She lay quietly and talked to Jesus about it. He would help her.

But even as she lay there, she heard soft footsteps again. Quietly she lay and listened and waited. Again her daughter came into view. The mother saw her reach up and put the orange back into the dish. Then the child stood still for a moment, patting her small hands together softly. "There, temptation!" her mother heard her say. "You thought you had me that time, didn't you?"

Then the child ran off to play, happy that she had won a victory in her own little way. Tears streamed down the mother's cheeks—glad tears—for she had gotten a glimpse of the strength of the structure she was building.

Children may sometimes fall into temptation; they may do things which conscientious parents have tried with all their strength to prevent. Parents should not be discouraged when their children fail. They should recall their own failures and remember that character-building requires perseverance, patience, and prayer.

One of the most honest children I ever knew was a little girl who attended one of the schools I taught. I could depend on Molly to tell me the truth. I knew that she would never resort to cheating. She was too conscientious for that.

Time and again she came and talked to me about her small difficulties and her efforts to live honestly. One time she told me of a trivial regulation she had unwittingly broken.

"I think I had better be punished for that," she told me soberly. "I need it."

It is hard to punish anyone like that.

One day a man was killed in an accident right in front of our schoolhouse. The children were all upset and nervous, for it happened at recess time and most of them saw it. I drew them in as quickly as I could. I decided to take advantage of the scare and reiterate how very dangerous it was for them ever to run into the street to retrieve a ball. They were very easy to impress then, but children do forget easily.

A week later, after a heavy winter rain, there came a hard freeze. The whole schoolyard was a glare of ice. The sidewalk from the schoolhouse to the street was as smooth and slick as glass. When I arrived, the children were sliding happily. But as I watched them, my heart jumped: their slide led right out onto the busy street. The curb added the thrill of a ski jump. The children were shouting with delight. Just then one lad flashed along the glassy incline and stopped right in the middle of the street. He narrowly escaped being hit by a passing car. With that, I had to forbid all sliding.

"But, teacher!"

"We'll be careful, honest; we won't go into the street anymore!"

"Please, please; nothing will happen!"

But I was adamant, for the danger was real. I went into the schoolhouse to get some ashes to put on the ice. When I returned a few minutes later, I saw three children go flying past on the forbidden sheet of ice.

"You had better stop, or the teacher will fix you," shouted a couple of the watching children.

"We don't care. She just doesn't want us to have any fun," they shouted back. At that, I called the youngsters in. I led them into my office. They stood there, the three of them, looking worried, defiant, and not a little bit sheepish.

I never punished children without having a talk with them. We discussed the situation frankly, and before we stopped, they were not only on my side, but were also telling me of harrowing accidents they knew about. They agreed that it was right for me to use the ruler on their hands. They knew that the rule I had made was only for their happiness and safety. They knew I loved them.

Just at this moment, the door of my office was cautiously opened, and two little hands were thrust toward me. It was Molly. Her face was drenched with tears.

"Rap my hands too, teacher," she sobbed. "I slid a couple of times, and it was a mean thing to do to you. I know you made that rule to keep us safe."

It was hard to rap her hands. I would rather have had my own beaten. But I knew at that moment that Molly had good stuff in her and that she would grow up to be a fine, caring, and responsible adult someday. And I was right.

Parents have to exercise great loving care when disciplining, else their harshness and lack of understanding will lead their children to deceit and lying. I know of a mother whose rules are so harsh and inviolable that her little boy has become a chronic liar.

Mother finds a vase broken on the floor. John knows he will be beaten if she finds he did it, even though it was done accidentally."

"Did you break that vase, John?"

"No, no. I didn't break it."

"Who did?"

"I don't know—maybe the cat."

"Oh, you did too! I know you did, for you were the last one in there. And I'm going to give you an extra thrashing for lying to me!"

How much better if that mother would recognize that other people—and children are people—have accidents and break things! If he had not actually been afraid, or if there had been any sort of understanding or confidence between the mother and son, the boy would have said, "Mom, I'm so sorry I broke your pretty vase! I really didn't mean to, but I was carrying that box through the room and my coat caught on it.''

The all-important thing is to have the friendship, love, and confidence of the children committed to our care. Ian MacClaran said, ''Be pitiful; everyone is having a hard time. Your little children will travel just as stony a road as ever you traveled. They need to be 'shod with the preparation' of the gospel of truth.''

A mother and father planned to go to a friend's house one night. They whispered all day so that little Eddie would not get wind of it. (I don't believe in that, either.) Finally the child got suspicious.

''Sissy said you were going to the Miller's house tonight. I wanna go.''

''No, Sissy will stay with you. We will give you a quarter to spend tomorrow.''

''I won't stay with Sissy. I am going with you.''

''All right, all right,'' agreed the mother. ''Then we won't go.'' She winked broadly at a visiting neighbor. ''You just go to bed. I'll stay right here with you.''

''Honest, Mamma?''

''Certainly, I won't go.''

In a few minutes the child was asleep, and the mother chuckled at how easily she had outwitted him. In a few minutes the parents were gone. Eddie did not learn about that particular deception, but he was reared in the midst of it, and became a master at the ''art.'' The mother weeps now and wonders and wonders where her child learned all his waywardness.

Is it wrong to lie to a child? It certainly is—one of the direst of wrongs. We parents stand in the place of God to our little ones. We interpret life—religion, behavior, happiness, good manners—to the open eyes and ears of our children. How much confidence would we have in God if we caught Him in lie after lie? What if we could not trust Him, could not believe in His promises?

Are you honest with your child? My old grandfather adored his children and grandchildren, and if anything went wrong he would threaten and threaten, but nothing ever came of it. His favorite threat was, "If I live till next Tuesday, I'll give you a hard thrashing!"

He would try to look at us sternly, but we would see his lips twitching behind his old duck blind of a beard. We well knew that next Tuesday would never come. But grandmother, ah! If she said, "You go out and get me a keen little switch," we knew what she meant. We could hide in the barn or the corncrib or behind the woodpile till the cows came home, but we knew we would get our switching, and a little interest besides, when we emerged, starving, sleepy, and penitent.

But we had confidence in grandma. Her hand might be swift to mete out just and righteous punishment, but it was wondrously soft and soothing when one was sick. It was capable, too, for had not we partaken of the crusty, succulent delicacies that flowed unendingly from her provident hands? We had confidence in grandma. It was on her shoulder that we would sob out our childish griefs and disappointment. We knew whom to believe.

The apostle Paul was so honest that when he believed it was his duty to persecute, not one did it more ardently than he. But when Jesus stopped his intolerant career midway, Paul was honest enough to see instantly that he was in the wrong and to seek to do the right thing even if it cost him his life.

He did not try to sneak out of the Philippian jail when the earthquake shook off his fetters and threw often all the doors. Something stood greater than liberty. A soul was at stake. He did not try to escape at the time of the shipwreck. He was too big, too magnanimous, for mean, petty advantages.

Even in Nero's prison house, Paul was strong in spirit and purpose. If there had been one grain of dishonesty left in his being, he could never have borne his extreme sufferings so magnificently. If he had collapsed of discouragement or weakness of purpose, all his fine experience on the Damascus road would have gone to nothing, and his years of toil would have been in vain. The significance of his whole life lay in his triumphant statement to young Timothy:

"I have fought a good fight, I have finished my course, I have kept the faith: henceforth there is laid up for me a crown of righteousness, which the Lord, the righteous judge, shall give me at that day: and not to me only [unselfish thought], but unto all them also that love his appearing."

Can your child learn this truth? Can he say, "I am trying with Jesus' help to fight a good fight. I want to finish my course nobly and keep faith with Jesus, so that there will be a crown of righteousness for me someday"?

He can and will say this if his parents are kind, loving, and scrupulously honest. But if the child and the mother connive to deceive the father; if the child and the father connive to deceive the mother; and if the child observes little disloyalties, petty dishonesties, lies, and evasions, what can the parents expect of the future? Parents who resort to dishonesty will awake someday, too late to retrieve what they have lost; and they will not find it again, though they seek it carefully with tears.

Strength, time, intellect, are but lent treasures. They belong to God, and it should be the resolve of every youth to put them to the highest use. . . . Every youth, every child, has a work to do for the honor of God and the uplifting of humanity."

—*The Adventist Home*, p. 280.

CHAPTER 5

Children Can Be Taught to Give

"One for Timmie, and one for me."

I was standing by the toy counter in a department store some years ago, when I saw a young father and mother come up to make a purchase. They bought their little 3-year-old girl a big tin horn. She give one ecstatic toot on it, then removed it from her pink mouth and held it out to the clerk in a dimpled hand. "Two little horns," she said in her high, sweet voice. "One for Timmie."

The clerk returned the big horn to the shelf, and handed the 3-year-old two smaller ones. The dainty little girl bestowed the other horn on her blinking, bewildered year-old brother in his buggy. He clutched it in a chubby hand and began sucking on it.

The mother caught my interested look. "She won't take anything without sharing it with the baby," she told me.

"How beautiful," I murmured. Then I went away whispering to myself these touching and very accurate lines from one of our best-known American poets:

> "Not what we give, but what we share,
>   For the gift without the giver is bare;
>   Who gives himself with his alms feeds three,

Himself, his hungering neighbor, and me."
        —JAMES RUSSELL LOWELL

Bless that generous little girl! I was fed. But I was fed up a little later in a doctor's office. A petulant child was making a nuisance of himself to all the patients in the waiting room. He gathered all the magazines and built a house with them in the middle of the floor. He went so far as to snatch some that patients were reading. The mother merely said patiently, "That isn't nice. We don't do that!"

He did not get mine. I held right on and looked him straight in the eye without cracking a smile. He let go without a word and went back to his pile. He knew whom he could "buffalo."

Later, when the mother left the office, her son gathered all the magazines up in his arms and marched right out with them. The mother whispered to the nurse, "I'll send them back as soon as I can divert his attention. It won't be half an hour."

Poor mother! She was that child's worst enemy. She was denying her child lessons of regard. Attitudes formed in babyhood are not soon outgrown. They snowball into gigantic proportions. The whole essence of God's plan to save the human race is found in the principle of utter unselfishness, in giving to others. Pity the poor child who is denied these lessons when his mind is young and while they can yet become part of his very being.

Some parents once asked my counsel about their willful, selfish, disobedient son. After some hesitation I told them what everyone already knew: Their son was so naughty and so rude that most of the children refused to play with him in or out of school. I told them that they must insist on prompt and exact obedience. They had started late, but perhaps it was not too late.

I told them that punishment must not be deferred, softened, or administered sporadically, but must come swiftly and surely when their commands, wishes, or rights were rudely disregarded.

They went away sad. They could not bear, they said, to

cross their dear son. He went into such rages when he was denied anything he wanted or when he was scolded! They did not dare to punish him! Why, the mother told me, he was sick for two days when she just tapped him a little for kicking grandma on the shins. He was so sweet, so precious, so good, when he was good. Did I not think he would outgrow it? I did not.

It is no kindness to rear a child in an atmosphere where he need not think of others, where he does not feel the deep, satisfying joy of giving. If such is the case in your home, you must create situations where the child must share, and teach him to like it. Teach him to sacrifice his own pleasures, and to have the deeper pleasure of seeing others happy.

When I was a teacher, I used to dine often with a large family with whom it was a pleasure to associate. I have seen the children of that family quietly count those who were at the table, then count the peach halves or pineapple slices so that they would take no more than their share. Those children had learned early that other people have rights. Teaching them so brought them no hardship, no deprivation. It was a kindness to teach them to live at peace with others.

One of the sweetest experiences in my life came when I was a teacher in a rural school. One tiny boy developed a terrible sore on his little face. His mother dressed it every morning, but for several days I had to change the dressing again during the day. I knew it hurt cruelly, and tried to do it as gently as I could. He would cling to me with his eyes all the time I worked on him.

A day or two after the ordeals were over, he came to class clutching a small parcel and his preprimer.

"I brought you something today," he said importantly. Carefully he unwrapped a small coach taken from his train set. I expressed pleasure over the gift, for indeed it did give me satisfaction. I was so happy because I had his tender little heart, not just that battered train car there in my hands. His eyes searched my face to see if I had spoken truly. His face cleared. He was satisfied. He sidled closer.

"Do you know," he whispered confidently, "I can read ever so much better if I sit on your lap?"

"Well, get right up here," I said, laughing. "We want you to learn to read quickly and well so that you can read stories to your grandma."

A friend of mine lived next door to a school where children from an orphans' home attended. Sometimes at recess or the noon hour some of the love-starved little ones would line the fence to watch my friend caring for her three small children on her front porch. She used to tell me that their sad little faces haunted her. They watched every move she made. One little fellow, bolder than the rest, came up on her porch one day. He rushed from place to place in a veritable riot of abandon, knocking over ferns and potted plants and shrieking with joy.

My friend was so outraged that she seized the youngster, forcibly conducted him outside the fence, and locked the gate. "I can't let a little boy come and play on my porch when he spoils all my things," she said.

He stood at the gate and looked at her soberly for a long time. Then he slowly turned and trudged off to the schoolhouse. Presently he returned. He held a grubby, dog-eared coloring book in his hand.

"Missus?" he called timidly.

My friend went to the door.

"I brought something for you," he said shyly.

My friend took the much-abused coloring book from his hand. Suddenly she realized that out of his poverty he had given the best he had. He was so poor that he had no other thing he could call his own. When she reached down and put her arms around him, he clutched her suddenly with thin arms and began to cry wildly.

"I didn't mean to hurt your things. I's s-s-sorry, for you know, I've never been in such a pretty place before."

He meant no wrong—he was only reveling, childlike, in the sunshine of love and abandon. He only needed to be taught.

Even as obedience is the core of character, so generosity is the very foundation of a happy life. But it is not enough to teach the child to give; the constant thought of others must be constantly pressed upon him. I think it pays to keep a notebook of stories that will make the imprint of this blessed virtue indelible on the child's character.

"Son, how did you get mud on your shirt?"

"Mel threw it on me. But I fixed him; I threw ink on him."

"Oh, I am sorry you did that, Jimmy. Did I ever tell you about the old Quaker farmer?"

"No, Daddy."

"He had a very cross, jealous neighbor. One day the neighbor came to see him. 'I found your horse in my pasture last night,' he said. 'Do you know what I did with it?'

" 'What did thee do with it, my friend?'

" 'I took it to the pound. And if I ever find any of your animals near my place again, I shall do the same thing.'

" 'Friend,' he said kindly, 'night before last I was wakeful. The moon was full, and it was almost as light as day. I got up and saw that your fence was broken down and your cattle were in my pasture. I repaired your fence. If it ever happens again, I shall do the same thing.'

" 'This so shamed the unfriendly neighbor that he went and got the good man's horse out of the pound and paid the dues himself."

Then the father addressed himself to his small son.

"Run over quickly now and get Mel's shirt, and we'll try to take out the ink spot. I think I have something in my workshop that might work."

Away ran Jimmy, eager and willing to make amends for ugliness. No wonder the greatest Teacher of all said, "Except ye . . . become as little children, ye shall not enter into the kingdom of heaven."

Smile, parents; smile, teachers. If your heart is sad, let not
your face reveal the fact. Let the
sunshine from a loving, grateful
heart light up the countenance.
. . . Adapt yourselves to the children's needs, and make them
love you. You must win their
affection, if you would impress
religious truth upon their heart.

—*Fundamentals of Christian Education*, p. 68.

CHAPTER 6

Children Can Be Taught to Worship

"Cindy, will you have prayer, please?"

While a father was nervously trying to read a chapter in worship one night, his two younger children ranged all over the room, gleefully conscious that they were the cynosure of all eyes. One had a fly swatter and was going systematically around the circle, giving everyone a sharp whack. I was not excepted. The other was playing on an old guitar. No one listened to the father's pitiful attempts to lead the family in the worship of God. The mother and the oldest child snickered constantly at the younger ones' antics. The children knew it, too. Even when we knelt to pray, none of us could be sure we would not be thumped. We were, several times. It is hard to worship in such an atmosphere.

Yet it is surely true, and has been proved true, that little children can be taught to sit still a few minutes a day to worship the heavenly King. It is one of the most valuable and fundamental things a child must learn. Beyond the gigantic expanse of stars and fleecy clouds lies a kingdom fairer than the morning and brighter than the day. God, the great embodiment of love and providence, is there. Jesus, the Saviour and Redeemer of the world, is there; and children should be taught about Him before their tender understanding can even grasp all that is spoken. It must be woven early into the tender fabric of the child's life, so that no part of the beautiful tapestry of his character can be godless or irreverent. Children will love the anticipation of heaven, and it will not be hard to teach them about Jesus.

Worship in a home where there are small children should never be long or tedious. Every day is a page in the children's lives. Every day, words are written on that page that affect souls and that mold them for time and eternity. Every day builds children into what they will ultimately be. Then let gentle words of prayer be written into the pages of their young lives, and the habit of prayer will become a part of them.

If the father and the mother want to read long chapters and carry on involved dissertations, let them do so at a time when the little ones are not present and required to sit still and listen. Some worships are so uninteresting that the children watch the clock and are ready to spring for freedom the moment the last amen has been uttered.

Yet it is the business—yes, business—of every parent to make the worship of God so sweet, so poignant, so lovely, that the children will be glad when it comes. Remember, they are being trained, bit by bit, day by day, morning and evening, to worship the Lord in the beauty of holiness.

I once knew a family that had a beautiful custom. When supper was ready every evening, the food was put in a place where it would keep warm for a few minutes, and the parents and children had worship around the table. Members of the family took turns conducting it. One evening it was 7-year-old Mike's turn. He led out in a song and asked his small sister to offer prayer. Then he read a story from a book that taught a lesson of honesty and truth. He laid aside the book and make a few remarks at the end of the story. He felt secure in doing so, for his family never laughed at his efforts. He had enough self-respect in his small person to feel sure that anything he might say would be soberly received. He himself offered the closing prayer. No wonder he is a successful individual today. He started young.

A certain father and mother were in the habit of using worship time to draw the attention of their children to the beauty of a glorious sunset, to a lovely flower, or to the blessings of God in the trees and grass. It was no wonder that the children thought often of God; they were taught to think of Him as the well-spring of all wisdom, all beauty, and all truth. Those parents spent half an hour teaching their little ones how cleverly God had fashioned a hand: fingers not all the same length; joints so fixed that one can pick up even the tiniest things! How cleverly fingernails are placed. Why the joints move a certain way. (There was a chorus of laughter as they tried to pick up things with stiff fingers and with their fingernails taped.) Children can indeed be taught to ponder on the love, the mercy and the wisdom of God.

Yes, indeed, children can be taught religion. They can be taught to worship. They can be taught to love to worship the King of heaven. But it takes time and patience and prayer and wisdom and long-suffering. It takes plans and searching and sweetness and constant admonition.

But if mothers and fathers prefer to squander their young parenthood in the marketplace of their own desires, and to entertain their selfish ambitions, they will vainly seek for one vestige of comfort for their heartache in their older days, for verily they shall not find it.

A noted criminal judge was lecturing on the frowning menace of lawlessness in this country.

"Parents are too selfish, too indolent, today to be the mothers and fathers of little children," he stated. "My parents did not send us to church when we were children. They took us. Moreover, father sat at one end of the pew, and mother sat at the other. There was a firm, kind guide—not a jailer—at both ends. We settled down to make the most of the service and to enjoy it. I have thanked God for that training a thousand times!"

An eminent chaplain in the central United States made a study in a large prison. There were 4,000 unfortunate men incarcerated there. He questioned every one of them about his home life and early training. Only one of that multitude of men—only one—confessed that his family had worship every day in his home. The 3,999 other men had been reared in a worshipless atmosphere. The chaplain further added that he was interested to note that the man who had had religious training in his home was later released, pardoned, and awarded a judgment for false arrest and imprisonment.

One of the greatest things in the teaching of religion is to begin even before the child can fully understand, and make worship grow with him into something ineffably precious and desirable. Make it a thing he cannot live without. You can do this if you put your whole soul into it. What in life is more important?

It is a beautiful thing when the little ones begin to formulate their own prayers. Often they will utter naive things that will sound distressingly funny, but it is fatal to laugh. Something will be lost that will be hard to regain. They will lose the sense of belonging to God. They will become self-conscious, and on the alert lest they become a laughingstock. Children like to be regarded as people with rights. Our Saviour issued warning after warning against offending one of His little ones. They are precious to Him.

A sweet 6-year-old felt security enough in her home to add her voice to the evening prayers of her family. She thanked God that Dombey, her big black pussycat, had such a long tail and could catch the mice in the basement so well. She thanked the Lord for her new doll buggy, and said that she was so glad that she did not have to sleep out in the alfalfa field, as did Moggy, the cow. "Bless father, mother, Billy, Jane, Moggy, and Dombey. Amen."

There must be nothing to spoil the sweet solemnity of the worship hour. If we could view the gropings of our children toward light as God must view ours—which are probably as foolish and ludicrous in His sight as our children's efforts may sometimes seem to us—fewer of our children would get discouraged and fall out by the way.

God grant that we as parents in a wicked and perverse generation will make the teaching of religion a living, moving, and beautiful thing in our home life; and that it will be a bridge that will span the dreadful abyss of sin and take our precious children to the very gates of God.

The essence of true politeness is consideration for others. The essential, enduring education is that which broadens the sympathies and encourages universal kindliness. That so-called culture which does not make a youth deferential toward his parents, appreciative of their excellences, forbearing toward their defects, and helpful to their necessities; which does not make him considerate and tender, generous and helpful toward the young, the old, and the unfortunate, and courteous toward all is a failure."

—*The Adventist Home*, p. 423.

CHAPTER 7

Children Can Be Taught to Be Good Guests

"Wow, I never swung on curtains before!"

Nearly everyone has a mental list of dreaded guests. Even an old black Persian cat that once owned us had a list. When we lived near a particularly rowdy group of children, poor old Blackie was once nearly pulled in two, and he became wary of this set of visitors. I heard the shouts of these children approaching our house one day, and as a low obbligato to their approach, I heard Blackie begin to growl. I saw him get up in his usual majestic way and survey our driveway down to the road. Sure enough, there came his enemies. He ran to the boys' bedroom, got into the closet, and slipped through a hole into the attic, where he remained until the children had gone home.

There are some child-guests who come to one's house confidently, buoyantly, and even joyously—and depart in the same frame of mind, leaving their hosts to survey the wreckage, lick their wounds, and try to recover their equilibrium and sanity. This is a pity, for every child has a right to be liked. Every child needs approval. He needs to develop the social side of his life. He needs to learn the skills of friendship. But he cannot make friends unless he is trained to regard the belongings of others as sacred to them, not as his to dismantle or destroy.

There are also moral reasons why a child should be taught these things. In the first place, destructiveness and wanton misuse of other people's possessions are a type of dishonesty. If a child is to develop into a person whom people will like and welcome, he must have a high regard for the "Thou shalt not steal" commandment.

Second, there is a danger in becoming impervious to the desires of others. It is wholesome to care what others think of what you do. A child is in a terrible state, fraught with grave danger, when he comes to the place where he does not care what you or anyone else thinks, so long as he can have what he fancies for the moment.

A neighbor boy named Tom came rushing into our house right after Christmas. When he left, our children's new toys were a shambles, and my wristwatch was in his pocket. I would have lost it had I not missed it just before he left, and suspecting him, based on his behavior, decided to look in his pocket as he was sidling out the door. Sadly, I could not invite him to come again to play with my boys. When he came again to my door, I told him gently that I was sorry, but he could not play with Bobby and Charlie, for he had not been a good guest the last time he came.

One day, Bobby brought a new friend named Lee home from school. Unfortunately, I happened to be at the grocery store when they arrived. When I got home only a few minutes later, even the curtains were torn from the windows! A vase was broken, and my children stood helpless in the doorway watching Lee tear around. They both burst out crying when they saw me.

"What is this?" I asked in a stern voice.

"Wow, I never swung on curtains before," answered unrepentant Lee, unabashed.

"You never will again here," I said quietly. I took him by the arm, propelled him gently but firmly to the front door. He was old enough to know how to behave, but either he had not been taught or he did not care. He saw that I was irate, but merely shrugged his shoulders. How callous and impervious! Later I saw him with his parents, and I understood. When they pleaded with him and begged him to do something, he refused. He hit his mother when she removed a forbidden object from his reach. Is there any wonder that she weeps now as she tells everyone that her son is worldly and never looks inside the church? When he was young and impressionable he did not learn to respect anyone, much less the dear Lord.

It is a great pity for a child's behavior to be so unpleasant that he is disliked, and finally banned from someone's home. I love children, and I hate to forbid any child from coming to see me. Children can be delightful guests and pleasant companions. The friendship of a child is one of the joys of life. When we lived in Africa my husband traveled considerably. Our boys were grown then, so I would often be alone. Once when he was to be gone, the mission doctor's little girls came and told me sweetly that they would be glad to stay with me, to keep me from being lonely. I was delighted, for they were lovely children, and a joy to have as guests. Amy came one night and Elizabeth the next. We developed a little routine for each evening.

First they would go with me to gather the eggs and shut up the chickens' pen. Then we would feed the monkey and the baboon and the little dog and the cat. By that time Andy, the cookboy, had supper on the table. We ate, then played hide-the-thimble in the living room.

After a while we would have a story hour, and tell each other stories by the fire until we both got sleepy. Then I would tuck the little girl into the big guestroom bed, with the mosquito netting draped all around it. After she got into bed there was one more story, and a funny poem. I used to amuse my own children this way, and Amy and Elizabeth loved it, too. I would tell some running story in rhyme, and the ridiculous way the rhymes came along would convulse us both with such laughter that we would be breathless by the time we were through. On the third day the girls' mother came to see me.

"Donnie is crying his little heart out," she said. "He wants to come and stay all night with you."

"Please, let him come," I laughed. That evening I saw a little 3-year-old coming across the yard, pulling a wagon in which were his pajamas and his slippers. He came running happily into my house, and together we began the evening's rigamarole. He laughed the whole time. Never once did I have to pry his small fingers out of some forbidden place. He had been taught at home how to behave, and was a model visitor.

Finally I dimmed the light and put the little fellow into bed. He snuggled down contentedly and smiled up at me. "Ain't it nice that I'm getting to hear stories and poems?" he said. I had to agree with him that it was really very nice. And it was. It was one of the sweetest parts of my mission life to make friends with the little children.

Jack the Predator

But when I was just a young girl we dreaded to see Mrs. Hall come to see us. She was always smiling, but little Jackie, her son, was always a few feet ahead of her, with a predatory look on his face. They no sooner got into the house than Jackie would start running all over to investigate. His mother did not even seem to see this, and she made no effort to restrain him.

We would look out the window, and someone would say, "Oh dear, here come Mrs. Hall and Jackie. Hurry and shut up the pantry. Put those ornaments away. Lock the study door. Fasten that cupboard."

I was usually detailed by my mother in a low whisper to follow and watch the child. It was not a pleasant chore. He would kick and bite me if I tried to protect anything from his investigating hands. I could hardly keep up with him.

Once I ran into the kitchen after him and found he had turned on all the gas burners, including the oven. I was kicked and bitten when I shut them off. I tried to lead him out into the yard, but he eluded me. He was into my father's desk next. In shutting a drawer, I accidentally pinched an inquisitive finger. Mrs. Hall came running to the rescue when his screams rose, far out of proportion to the small hurt.

"She hurt me; she hurt me," he screamed, pointing at me.

"Oh, darling, let mamma kiss it," cooed Mrs. Hall, giving me an unpleasant look. "You just come in here with mother, where you won't be hurt."

"I don't want to," he declared. "Make her go away."

My mother interposed at that. "I told her not to let anyone get into daddy's desk," she said. "You come into the living room, Jackie. You can play in there."

He cried and screamed so hard that his mother finally took him home. We all were glad to see them go, for it had been an exhausting afternoon for us. Yet, it was a pity. Little Jackie would have been happier if he had been shown how a guest should behave. It is part of a child's birthright to learn the grace and beauty of being a lovely guest. It is a good thing for him to learn that not everything even in his own home is for him to handle and play with. I used to tell my small boys, "This is not yours. It is mine. You have your things, and you must not bother my things."

A child who is permitted to rummage in any drawer, paw through mother's purse, get into aunt's or sister's things, is likely to be a nuisance as a guest.

How are you training your children? Teach them how to behave when they are guests. They have a right to be liked, to be welcomed, to be asked to come again. It is your fault if they are dreaded guests. A child is happier if he has learned the lesson of self-control.

Treat your family in a manner
that Heaven can approve, and so
that peace may be in your dwelling . . ."

—Testimonies, vol. 2, p. 86.

CHAPTER 8

Children Can be Taught to Love God

"Please don't tell anyone I told you this . . ."

I think I hate my father," a sweet-faced young girl named Lisa confided to me, when she had stayed after school one day for a private talk. I tried not to look shocked, as she went on to explain.

"Please don't tell anyone I told you this," she pleaded. "It would embarrass my parents." Mom feels so bad about the way things are in our home and she doesn't want us to talk about it. But sometimes I think I'll go crazy if I don't tell someone. I know I'm supposed to respect my father. I don't like feeling the way I do, but I don't know what to do about it."

We talked a long time that lovely fall afternoon, weeping and praying together. She said softly, "You know, my dad is a deacon in the church. And I read this week in Bible class that deacons should not be doubled-tongued. That's what hurts me. Dad's tongue says one thing at church, but at home it says something else."

I took Lisa's hand in mine. My heart went out to her. I knew more about her father than I revealed. The whole town knew about his insane fits of temper. It was common knowledge that the family's oldest son, Dan, had run away from home at 14, because of his father's harsh treatment.

Lisa told me about her brother to unburden her heart.

Her young face was wet with tears as she told me of the terrible scene that had taken place just before Dan left home.

"My father yelled at him, belittled him, and made fun of him once too often. Dan screamed that he hoped he would die before he ever went into a church again. We have never seen him since. Mother often cries in the night. I have heard her."

I pondered this awful situation, this father, so unkind, with a temper so unbridled as to spoil his children's lives for time and perhaps eternity.

"If any man among you seem to be religious, and bridleth not his tongue, but deceiveth his own heart, this man's religion is vain" (James 1:26).

Too many men and women have a religion that shows up beautifully at church, but which wears thin at home. They depend on the ones at home to forgive them continually, and to tolerate the ugliness they show so often toward those they love. The servant of the Lord has written:

"Treat your family in a manner that Heaven can approve, and so that peace may be in your dwelling. . . . Your children have had your bad example before them; you have blamed, and censured, and manifested a passionate spirit at home, while you would, at the same time, address the throne of grace, attend meeting, and bear testimony in favor of the truth. These exhibitions have led your children to despise you and the truth you profess. They have no confidence in your Christianity."—*Testimonies*, vol. 2, p. 86.

Reaction on children

There are in every place people who have not overcome the wickedness in their own lives, and whose families see all too much of their temper fits and tantrums. We are told that the very expression on the countenance has an influence for good or for evil. Parents who would never lay a hand on their children thoughtlessly destroy their self-esteem with angry words.

Children are damaged by these harsh and hateful words, just as surely as they are bruised by blows and kicks.

The Bible says, "Fathers, provoke not your children to anger, lest they be discouraged."

One father I knew had fanatical ideas about the proper way to dress, and he rode this hobbyhorse continually. You could not talk to him for five minutes without his beginning to recite the failings of all the church members, arrogantly proclaiming the ultimate destination of those who did not comply with what he felt were the proper standards of dress. His wife and daughters were miserably ashamed of his belligerent attitude. They were always dressed modestly and in good taste. But, of course, even they did not in any way please this man. He thought flat shoes were the only kind a Christian woman should wear; and as for the vulgarity of displaying the knees—well, a person who did that was headed for perdition!

One day he sighed in my presence and intoned loudly that he could hardly hope to do a thing with his own household when the minister's wife wore such vulgar attire. The minister's wife was a friend of mine, and no one could dress more modestly than she, and she would have been crushed if she had heard his unkind remarks so entirely unwarranted.

Everyone felt sorry for his wife and daughter, and you can be sure the girls escaped from home as soon as they could by way of early and ill-considered marriages. Both have been gone from the church for years now; gone from a religion they never saw demonstrated in their home and that was never made attractive.

"Pray for my son, please," said a father to me one day in a most pious manner. "He tells lies; he lies when the truth would serve his purpose better. He'll lie when he can't help knowing that I know he's lying; he'll brazen it out no matter what I do or say."

I might have replied:

"I could tell you why he lies, friend. The whole church knows how you chew that poor boy out. You may think your harangues go unnoticed, but they do not. Your neighbors see your wife leaving her house and going out into the garden to weep and sob because of your hateful tirades.

Your son hides from you when your brow clouds over, and lies at the slightest pretext in the vain hope of avoiding your wrath.

"Your violent fits of anger will mean your eternal destruction unless you overcome them by the grace of God. If you do not put this failing in God's hands, and ask for His help in overcoming it, all your piety in the church and your missionary activities on weekends will not save you, and you will continue to drag your family down with you.

"Admit your sin to God, and with His help, humbly ask your family for forgiveness. It will take some time, but if you put your trust in God's power—He will give you the wisdom and strength to rebuild your relationship with your wife and son. God will save you from your terrible temper, and through you, save your beautiful young boy from a life time of misery and give him back his self-esteem."

Children can be taught to love God and to delight in worshiping Him. But this must be taught by example. Pious mouthings in church do not impress children who have been subjected to constant harangues at home. If you do shout unkind words in anger at your children—and who doesn't, at times—humbly ask them for forgiveness. Teach them, by your example, that even though human beings, including parents, are not perfect, God loves us anyway, and shows us how to love and forgive each other.

Though all are precious in His sight, the rough, sullen, stubborn dispositions draw most heavily upon His sympathy and love; for He traces from cause to effect. The one who is most easily tempted, and is most inclined to err, is the special object of His solicitude.

—Counsels on Sabbath School Work, pp. 178, 179.

CHAPTER 9

Children Can Be Taught Good Behavior on Vacations

"You should have seen us hurry and get out of there!"

The Marywell family were going on a vacation. For months, they had planned just where they would go, and where they would stop, and what they expected to see. But alas, both parents and children were a poorly disciplined lot, and they spread dismay and desolation wherever they went. Relatives were sorry to see them arrive and glad to see them go, but the Marywells never seemed to sense this. They got into trouble at several motels because of the noise and loud talk and late-night running about that went on. A manager at one place came twice to ask them to be quiet.

"Of all the nerve!" Mrs. Marywell said angrily, when he had gone. "We paid a fortune for this place, and they want us to be still as the grave!" And the children were listening.

To them, naturally, mother's utterances were exactly right, and if she said they were being unfairly treated, the children believed it. Their parents were leading them to believe, by their example and by their very words, that they were free to do whatever they wished, regardless of the rights of others.

The Marywells stopped at one motel late in their trip. They brought their luggage in, and after the usual shouting and running up and down the halls, finally settled down for the night. The children were in bed, all but 7-year-old Martin, who persisted in turning on and off a big china lamp on a table beside the bed. He jabbed the button on the lamp's base so roughly it was a wonder he did not knock the lamp off the table.

Mother and Father Marywell behaved as though they did not see what he was doing. They sat and read and talked and looked at television, just as if everything their son was doing was perfectly all right. Yet, a lamp is not, was not, and never will be, a plaything. Martin should have learned that at home. Even Martin, however, couldn't keep up his boorish behavior all night, and eventually drifted off to sleep.

The next morning, while the family was busily getting packed up to leave, Martin discovered a renewed fascination for the china lamp. Jab, jab, jab went Martin's small fingers on the lamp's on-off button. Once more, Mother ignored Martin's activity. Father was busy packing the car.

Suddenly, *crash!* The big vase-lamp lay on the floor, smashed in pieces.

Mrs. Marywell stopped her packing and shrieked at the child, "Now, just look what you've done, Martin! Just see! Now, you just march and get that big wastebasket. Clean it all up before Daddy sees it. And now we'll have to get right out of here or we're going to have to pay for that lamp. That'll cost a lot of money, and money doesn't grow on trees!"

All the children were listening, for little Jean told several people about it when they got home. "You should have seen us hurry and get out of there," she confided. "We had the car all packed in a few minutes time, and we didn't have to pay for that lamp."

What a lesson in dishonesty those children learned that day—a lesson in conniving too; a lesson in deceit; a lesson that will make it harder in a hard world for those little children to find the path to life eternal.

"Honesty should stamp every action of our lives. Heavenly angels examine the work that is put into our hands;

and where there has been a departure from the principles of truth, 'wanting' is written in the records."—*Counsels on Stewardship*, p. 142.

Someday the Marywells, with their children, must stand before the judgment bar of God. There will be before them the gate of heaven, with the ineffable glory of eternity shining through, beckoning with a joy unspeakable to the sweetness of an endless life with Christ and the redeemed who have washed their robes. But to allow vases, lies, lamps, and rude behavior to bar that gate would be a frightful tragedy.

A child's character is warped by the continual repetition of such experiences as the one just mentioned. He should be taught at home to respect the property of others. It is the duty of parents to show him, by their example, the importance of this. Thus led, he can learn to be discerning, observant, full of grace and sweetness.

"Some parents allow their children to be destructive, to use as playthings things which they have no right to touch. Children should be taught that they must not handle the property of other people. For the comfort and happiness of the family, they must learn to observe the rules of propriety. Children are no happier when they are allowed to handle everything they see. If they are not educated to be caretaking, they will grow up with unlovely, destructive traits of character."—*Child Guidance*, pp. 101, 102.

Trips can be a blessing to children whose parents are in the habit of teaching them to follow the blessed Jesus. They can be drawn nearer to the kingdom of heaven than ever before. This sweet fellowship of family togetherness, combined with the excitement of travel to new places can run like a golden thread through the very fabric of their characters. Integrity, kindness, and love will bring the family into oneness with Christ. During the long hours of travel, by loving counsel, by example, by story, and by precept the children can learn more surely the way to the kingdom.

"Let parents and children remember that day by day they are each forming a character, and that the features of this character are imprinted upon the books of heaven. God is taking pictures of men and women, transferring the features of the face to the polished plate. What kind of picture do you wish to produce? Parents, answer the question! What kind of picture will the great Master Artist make of you in the records of heaven?"—*Ibid.*, p. 562.

Sharp words and continual censure bewilder the child, but never reform him. Keep back that pettish word; keep your own spirit under discipline to Jesus Christ; then you will learn how to pity and sympathize with those brought under your influence.

—Counsels on Sabbath School Work, p. 125.

CHAPTER 10

Children Can Be Taught Good Behavior While Shopping

"Hide this quickly, while he's not looking."

This lovely and careful business of getting children ready for life should include teaching them the grace of good manners in stores and other places of business. Here an untrained child, a bundle of curiosity filled with the natural childish desire to handle everything, can become a dreaded nuisance. Here, also, children can be tempted to violate the "Thou shalt not steal" commandment. If in a child's own home he is permitted to play with anything he can reach or touch, he is bound to consider everything "fair game" in stores and other public places.

Parents who, out of a desire to solve a problem in an easier way, put out of reach or hide things they do not want their children to have, unwittingly give their children the idea that anything they *can* reach is theirs by way of discovery. I have met many children who had this idea; and they learned it at home.

Parents often say, "Hide this quickly, while he's not looking." It may be harder and it may involve a little difficulty at first, but if a child learns by a word that some things are just not his, he will be a happier child than if he is turned loose on everything. A child's natural restless acquisitiveness needs parental bounds.

One day his grandmother saw my little son, Charlie,

eyeing a pretty, expensive vase on a low table. "I'll put it up so he won't break it," she said.

"Oh, no, Mom, " I told her, "please don't. Come here, Charlie," I interrupted myself to say. The baby came to me, on his shaky little legs, smiling happily.

I took his little hand and led him to the vase.

"That is Grandma's pretty vase," I told him. "Charlie must not touch it, for it might break."

He looked up into my face. "Charlie not touch?" he asked.

"No," I said. "Charlie must not touch."

He toddled away and played with something else, but soon the vase caught his eye once more. One small, fat finger extended, he approached the vase again. Then he stopped and looked at me. "Not touch?" he asked. "No," I said gently but firmly. He backed away from the forbidden object and did not bother it any more. Grandma marveled at it, but it was not so wonderful. Charlie and I had talked of such things in that way for a long time, and he understood me perfectly. He knew what I meant when I said he must not touch. And he was not unhappy.

In stores children reveal their home training. Whenever possible, parents should accompany their children to stores. Children should be instructed to look—yes, look all they want to—but not to touch unless they are invited to do so by the clerk. It is a part of the training of a child in the graces of life to be well-mannered in stores. Here he may witness to the refining influence of the truth of the Lord Jesus Christ.

I used to make up stories to explain the different things I wanted to teach my boys when they were small. Little rhymes helped too.

"The things in stores are not yet yours; Keep hands away until you pay," we'd say together in the car on the way to the store.

I took some neighborhood children to a hardware store one day. They had begged me to take them with me. But as soon as they got in the door they began to chase one another all around, whirling and flying from one aisle to another. I called them to me.

"You must not do that," I said. "This is a store, not a racetrack. You are bumping into people and making a nuisance of yourselves."

"Oh, Mama doesn't care," the oldest one assured me. "She always lets us."

I told them that if they wanted to be with me, they could not do this, for people do not like it. I pointed out that even the manager was standing up to look. I showed them that a clerk nearby was watching. "You must always watch to see whether you are doing something that is not polite," I told them. "Get the habit of watching. That is a part of growing up. You would not want to be told to leave this store, would you?"

The children thought that over. "I guess not," the oldest child decided. "I might want to come back." The others nodded, and their behavior in the store improved.

Last summer I was eating lunch in a large drugstore near a university when a dozen or so teenagers came in. They were all around fourteen or fifteen years old. There were both girls and boys, and they filled about three tables. I noticed that the women who waited on the tables were very nervous, and one called the manager over.

"Get out of here, every one of you," he commanded. "And you're lucky I don't call the police and have you all arrested!"

They grumbled and loudly shoved their chairs around, but got up and left, and stood out in front of the store talking. It was a hot day, and perhaps they wanted a cool drink or some ice cream, but their bad behavior of the day before had closed at least one door.

"You should have seen the mess they made of the tables yesterday when they came in," a waitress volunteered to me. "They emptied salt into the sugar, filled the salt shakers with Coca Cola, and broke nine glasses. It took a long time to clean up after them."

Such young people have not learned the first principles

of courtesy and politeness, or to respect the rights of others. The unpleasantness they cause is nothing, compared to the unhappiness their own behavior causes them.

Let us, then, as Christians teach our children the refining nature of real religion. "One child, properly disciplined in the principles of truth, who has the love and fear of God woven through the character, will possess a power for good in the world that cannot be estimated."—Ellen G. White in *Signs of the Times*, July 13, 1888.

Children should pray for grace to resist the temptations which will come to them—temptations to have their own way and to do their own selfish pleasure. As they ask Christ to help them in their life service to be truthful, kind, obedient, and to bear their responsibilities in the family circle, He will hear their simple prayer.

—*The Adventist Home*, p. 299.

Children Can Be Taught to Treat Others With Respect

"My mother says I don't have to."

The little face was pitiful. How it tugged at my heart-strings. It brought tears to my eyes. Big tears also brimmed in the sweet brown eyes.

"But, Mama, I am your own little boy and you love me. You won't punish me, will you?" The little voice was so sweet, and the fat little fingers patted my hand in childish conciliation.

I would rather have said to him, "Well, Bobby, I'll let you go, this time. But you must never do it again." But I did not dare do this. It was a building block in his little character. He needed to learn to be depended on and to learn to obey. To have changed my mind about punishing him would have destroyed his confidence in my word.

Bobby had been told several times to come straight home from the store. He had been told why, and had been told that at nightfall the streets are not safe for children. The traffic is heavier, and the evil in the cities is great.

But he had not heeded. He had again stopped to play, and he had played so long that we were worried about his safety and had been out hunting for him. I had told him before, that the next time he did this he would have to be punished. For his own sake I must do what I had told him I would do. It was not easy, but it was the only right thing to do.

His punishment helped him to remember, for a child must learn the "Thou shalt's" and the "Thou shalt not's" of the home. Then he will not chafe at the rules of the school and of the church and of the Lord.

"In allowing children to do as they please, parents may think themselves affectionate, but they are practicing the veriest cruelty. Children are able to reason, and their souls are hurt by inconsiderate kindness, however proper this kindness may be in the eyes of the parents. As the children grow older, their insubordination grows. Their teachers may try to correct them, but too often the parents side with the children, and the evil continues to grow, clothed, if possible, with a still darker covering of deception than before. Other children are led astray by the wrong course of these children, and yet the parents cannot see the wrong. The words of their children are listened to before the words of teachers, who mourn over the wrong."—*Child Guidance*, p. 326.

From the moment the child shows his small, earnest, shy, mischievous, or self-centered face in the schoolroom, he is a living display of the manners he has learned in his home. Parents would be terribly embarrassed if they could see how nearly their children carry to school the imperfections of the home.

"Let me help you," Benjamin said to his teacher shyly. She was sweeping out the entry of the school. He took the broom and carefully finished the small chore. There was real pleasure glowing on his small, earnest face.

She knew by this that Benjamin was in the habit of helping his mother and his father at home. He had been taught to be alert to things to do. And he had been praised for doing them. Later when the teacher visited in the home, Benjamin was on the job, doing his chores. He fed the cat, took out the garbage, and filled the woodbox next to the fireplace.

"Anything else, Mom?" he asked, brushing the bark slivers from his sweater sleeves.

"No, thank you, Ben," his mother said. "You've already been a big help. You may go and play now." Benjamin grinned from ear to ear at the warm words of praise and scampered out to play, his good impulses once again reinforced by a loving and wise mother.

John Was Different

But it was not the same with John, a student in my school room during my first year of teaching. He was a trial everywhere. He was known as a bully. He teased the little ones, and took their things from them, and threw their small toys so he could watch them run after them. His uproarious laughter at their expense was not a lovely thing to hear.

On the playground he was an especial trial. Large for his age, he seemed to wear a perpetual, dissatisfied scowl on his face. I always played with the children, and I noticed right at the beginning of the school year that the other children did not choose him for their side until the very last. I was to learn why very soon.

One day we started a game of prisoner's base. John got caught early in the game, and the trouble began right then.

"No fair, no fair," he shouted. "You ganged up on me. I ain't goin' to prison. I ain't." He marched right back to the line, his lower lip stuck out defiantly. I had seen the whole thing. He had been honestly caught.

"Do you mean you are not going to play?" I asked.

"Oh, yes, I'll play," he said. "But they're not supposed to catch me. I never take 'it.' My mother says I don't have to."

"Perhaps your mother does not know how this game works," I told him. "In this game, if you are not willing to be caught and go to the prison, you cannot play. Those are the rules of the game. You can sit on the steps and watch us, if you don't want to play."

John opened his mouth to speak, a look of incredible surprise spreading over his face. Then, looking at my face, he changed his mind. He stood for a moment and looked at me, and I looked at him. "Aw right," he said in a low voice, "I'll go to prison."

Then the game became happy and uproarious. I was the one to tap him and get him out of prison. Later, when I got in prison, he sneaked around and got me out. When we ran back to the line together, he said, "Boy, I like to get caught; I didn't know it was so much fun."

"Mrs. Edwards, you're in for it now," an eighth-grader told me later. "He'll go home and tell his mother, and she'll call you up and tell you off tonight. She always tells the teachers off if they do anything to John."

I decided to talk to the children awhile after the recess about the value of playing the game. I told them that games are for recreation, for exercise. As we play them we must not care whether we win or lose, but have a good time. Someone must lose or the whole pattern of the game is lost. Life is like a game, I told them. Sometimes we lose, sometimes we win, but we can play the game and be happy in it all.

I told them that Jesus loved them and wanted them to be happy. I told them how, when He was on this earth, he had lived to bless others, and how as a child He was full of grace and truth. I read to them from my favorite book on the life of Christ: "The aged, the sorrowing, and the sin-burdened, the children at play in their innocent joy, the little creatures of the groves, the patient beasts of burden,—all were happier for His presence. He whose word of power upheld the worlds would stoop to relieve a wounded bird."—*The Desire of Ages*, p. 74.

Then I told the children that Jesus cared about the quality of their lives, and that he wanted them to grow up to be shining examples of His love. "If we are thoughtless and hateful when we are children, "It is likely that we will be spoiled and hateful when we are grown." I told them about miserable men and mean old women I had known, and how unhappy they were because they had never learned how sweet it is to get along with other people. "We must strive to overcome the selfish tendencies in our lives while we are young, or they will set like cement, and it will be difficult to change when we are older," I continued. "That is the reason that being converted is a miracle. The Lord does something that is really impossible. He takes an ugly, hateful life and makes it into something lovely and beautiful," I concluded.

I was distressed to see the significant glances the children cast in John's direction during my talk. His infamous reputation was a cruelty his parents had inflicted upon him. He had a right to the pleasure of popularity and happy associations and fellowships. But he had never tasted those joys. Selfishness and his parents' unwise love had set him apart as an oddity, and not a pleasant one at that. When the other children laughed and played together, he could only look on sadly, for he honestly did not know how to get along with them. But he was young, and the desire to change had been awakened in him. Slowly he began to learn how to get along with others. My experience with John, and others like him during my years of teaching, convinced me that it is never too late for the power of Jesus' love to work on young hearts—and that loving training and example can help even the worst bully.

To act from impulse in governing a family is the very worst of policy. . . . How unjust it is to put years and maturity of strength against a helpless, ignorant little child! Every exhibition of anger on the part of the parents confirms rebellion in the heart of the child.

—*Signs of the Times*, April 30, 1984.

CHAPTER 12

Children Can Be Taught to Call Sin by Its Right Name.

"A fella has a right to one, once in a while."

Sin is heinous and horrible. It separates us from our loving God. Its wages are death; its end is death; its rewards are paltry and lying; its promises are deceitful and turn to ashes in our very hands.

How can we teach children the ugliness of sin? Since sin is transgression of God's law, we must first teach our children to be law-abiding creatures, to love and obey the law—the law of God and of government. We can begin by teaching them the reasonableness of the rules that govern our households and the utter desirability of adhering to them for their own safety and well-being.

Too many children are dealt with in a casual or off-hand way when they transgress, so calmly that they feel guilty of nothing. The impression on the child is, "Oh, I did not do such a bad thing." This is not the way to teach the exceeding sinfulness of sin. It is minimizing it and soft-pedaling it, and the child is lulled into a sense of false well-being when he should be facing the experience of changing his ways. When a child obeys the rules, cheer him on, affirm him, let him see that you recognize his effort. When rules are broken, let him know you are very concerned.

To let a child see you are deeply disturbed by his behavior, to let him see that he is treading on exceedingly dangerous ground if he repeats the offense, is most salutary. A child measures his offense by the attitude you take toward it. He has no other yardstick. I used to watch my father's face when I did something I shouldn't. If I saw the bone along his jaw turn white and his lips thin to a line, an icy hand gripped my heart. My dread was painful, but wholesome. I knew that my father loved me, because he told me often. I knew that he loved me just as much, even when I transgressed. But I also knew that he expected obedience. When he punished me, I knew I had done wrong. I trusted my father's judgment. He had discussed the rules with me, and I knew they were for my own protection and well-being. He was right. I was wrong.

It is the tempter's plan to make sin seem trivial and to belittle it. He is ever striving to make the pathway to transgression easy and inviting. It is the parent's duty, with loving firmness, to let the child know that sin cannot go unpunished. The punishment should, of course, fit the offense.

Sin can tie you up and bind you round and round until every cell screams because of the chains that grow always stronger. And sin can blind a human being until it seems the natural thing, the usual thing. Eyes perverted by sin need the scales dropped from them, or they can never see straight or clearly again. Only heavenly eyesalve will do it.

Sin is prolific: one sin spawns a million more— swarming, blinding, binding sins. And the hardening power of sin! The conscience finally becomes like cement. Let's teach children to stay away from it. It is death.

Gene Mersho occasionally helped himself to money left on the dresser by his father. His mother admonished him for it, but did not let his father know what he was doing. He established a habit of coveting and taking what belonged to others. If Carol, his sister, left a candy bar in her school bag, Gene got it. Carol told on him, but nothing came of it. He decided his parents didn't care if he took things or not. He became calloused to the habit.

Passing a fruit store on his bicycle daily, he learned to be clever at filching applies. "They charge too much," he told his hardened conscience. "A fella has a right to one once in a while." The conviction grew. He had those apples coming to him. His fingers became exceedingly clever.

His parents sent him to a boarding school. He was popular, and the girls liked him. He was good at sports. But he took his habit with him.

The fellows on his floor began to complain. Their candy, apples, oranges, pencils, pens, and typing pads disappeared. Soon a watch was missing.

In no time, the entire dormitory was in an uproar, with boys accusing each other of thievery. Fortunately, the dean was a resourceful fellow who also cared deeply about the boys in his charge. He kept both eyes open at all times, as deans must do. He had begun to suspect that affable, popular Gene had a problem with stealing. One evening, while the other boys were gone to supper, he invited Gene to have a little visit with him in his apartment.

After some preliminary pleasantries, he gently broached the subject: "Gene, I've been watching you pretty closely the last week or so. Actually, I've been watching everybody—trying to puzzle out why so many of the boys' possessions seem to be disappearing. And on a couple of occasions, I've noticed some things in your possession that looked suspiciously like some of the missing objects. So this afternoon, I played a little trick on you. I put a candy bar in plain sight on the top of Jim Ivey's dresser, and left the door open. I guess you know what happened after that, Gene."

Gene hung his head. "Big deal, a candy bar," he mumbled. But the dean wasn't about to let him brush it off so lightly. Firmly he stated his opinion of stealing, whether the object stolen was large or small. Then he changed the subject, and began to talk about all the good things he had noticed about Gene—how much the other boys liked him, how good he was at sports, how helpful he had been when the whole dorm had painted old Mrs. McDuff's house for her over the spring holidays.

"Gene," he said, "You are too fine a person to ruin your life because of one weakness. Jesus wants more for you than that. I think there are some other stealing incidents that you ought to tell me about." And he continued, looking Gene straight in the eye, "Stealing is a sin. It's a terrible way to treat God and your fellow students. But you can make it right. God will forgive you if you confess your sins and ask Him to. And the other fellows will forgive you too, if you tell them you're sorry and do everything you can to make it right."

Something broke loose in Gene. The confessions came tumbling out. Soon the two of them were on their knees, Gene with tears running down his young face, the dean with his arm around the boy's trembling shoulders.

With the dean's support and understanding, Gene began to make things right. He returned all the possessions he had taken, and promised to make restitution where things could not be returned. He asked for his friends' forgiveness, and to his amazement, he didn't lose their friendship. In fact, some of them seemed to gain a new respect for him. And the important thing is that he gained a new respect for himself.

It certainly is not love for a child that shields him and minimizes his wrongdoings. It is moral laxness and a cowardly laziness that falter at issues that can be life and death matters. It is sentimentalism that toys with sin, and allows it to ruin young lives.

Weakness and vacillation on the part of a parent will only worsen the situation. Bribes and coaxing are no answer, either. The child learns to bargain, to haggle, to sell to the highest bidder. He never gains the concept of doing right for right's sake. Misconceptions grow like poisonous plants. It will take some doing to uproot them. To neglect the child's earliest training, and consequently to strengthen wrong tendencies, makes his after-education more difficult and causes discipline to be too often an extremely painful process.

You, the parents, can lighten this blow, if only you will.

*well-ordered Christian
household is a powerful argument
in favor of the reality of the
Christian religion—an argument
that the infidel cannot gainsay.
All can see that there is an influence at work in the family that
affects the children, and that the
God of Abraham is with them. If
the homes of professed Christians
had a right religious mold, they
would exert a mighty influence
for good. They would indeed be
the "light of the world."*

—*The Adventist Home*, p. 36.

CHAPTER 13

Children Can Be Taught Good Behavior in Restaurants

"I've seen too many people hungry."

Anyone who has served food at camp meeting, junior camp, or in a cafeteria anywhere sometimes wishes fervently that some children could have a little more training in proper conduct before eating in a public place. There it can be seen just what kind of training children have had. And while many children have been taught excellent table manners, others show a woeful lack in this area.

When children paw through the bread in search of some slice they fancy, when they reach far over other food to get the biggest piece of cake or the biggest apple, one can be sure that someone has failed to set a good example and teach these children the principles of gracious living.

It is a never-ending task, an exacting chore, to train children to do the lovely and proper thing. Too often the child has been in a home where the manners of one or both of the parents have left a great deal to be desired. Or many times the family never sits down together to eat, and there is no setting in which the children can learn the arts and graces of good table manners. Pity the poor child who has never been in company with people who show him, by their example, how to do things the right way.

Some children have never been taught not to heap their plates with food. Confronted with a cafeteria line or a table full of food at a church dinner, they greedily take more than they need, pick at it, play with it, and go away leaving more on their plates than they should have eaten in two meals. My father used to say, "Take only a little, and if you want more you can take it later. I don't want to see a lot of good food wasted and thrown out. I've seen too many people hungry."

Left to his own devices, a child will heap a tray full of food in a cafeteria, pleading all the time for this and that, until he has more than he can possibly eat. With his parents' example and guidance, the child can learn to exercise good judgment and self-control in the cafeteria line.

Thirteen-year-old Jean went through the academy cafeteria line every day and handled this and that until she found the biggest and best dish of food for herself. Poor Jean came to academy handicapped by a lack of training. Far from making her happy, her unpleasant manner and thoughtless behavior hampered her ability to make new friends and made it difficult for her to learn to live happily in her new situation.

No one can live to himself. Children will grow up and go out and meet a world that often is not too kind. A child needs an armor of gentle training in doing the right things to help him live happily in a world that is hard to conquer at best. Being a polite and thoughtful Christian is one of the best ways we have to witness to others about what the love of Jesus has done in our hearts.

Because we are an "epistle . . . , known and read of all men," we need to exercise great care and caution lest we take the name of the Lord in vain. "The Lord will not hold him guiltless that taketh his name in vain."

With a firm, kind, considerate hand, hold the lines of government, guiding and control-
ling their minds and purposes,
yet so gently, so wisely, so lov-
ingly, that they will still know
that you have their best good in
view.''

—*Counsels to Parents, Teachers and Students*, p. 335.

CHAPTER 14

Children Can Be Taught Good Habits

"I think you would like some Ovaltine, wouldn't you?"

Every time I go to the home of a friend, her son, Jamie, welcomes me as warmly as she does. He smiles, runs to take my coat and purse, and does all he can to see that I am comfortable. Though he is only five, Jamie has a rare grace for so small a child.

Only yesterday as I was visiting with his mother, he came and patted me gently on the knee to get my attention, and looking up into my face, said, "I think you would like a nice cup of Ovaltine, wouldn't you Mrs. Edwards?" I could not resist that, and he eagerly ran to prepare it for me—with his mother's help.

Children need to be taught to graciously greet a guest. They are a part of the home, and their training is deficient if it is lacking in this social grace.

When children come in from play or from school or from an errand, it is rude and inconsiderate for them to dash through the house, paying no attention whatsoever to a guest in the home. Many children come in shouting, slamming doors, demanding, and never give a guest so much as a glance.

This should not be, for the child will always need the grace of meeting people. Much of his future happiness and success will depend upon such small niceties. Public relations are important, and these principles cannot be learned in a minute. Beauty of behavior comes from years of careful training in the art of being gracious.

It is a pleasant and rewarding experience to meet a family of well-trained, well-mannered children. Every time I go to a certain home, even if I am unexpected, the children run to meet me almost before my car is stopped. Little Amanda will say, all out of breath, "You can stay for supper, can't you?"

And Jimmy's eyes will be shining when he says, "Wow, I like to see you come!"

Needless to say, I love to visit in that home. The children want me to see their new books, their pets, their hobbies, and their games.

I am convinced that these lovely traits of character do not crop up by accident; they represent days and months and years of parental example, guidance, and training, and the product is a delight to behold.

In some homes, when visitors are there, the children seem to think they must be seen and heard continually. They will pound on the piano and scream and run through the house to such an extent that the hosts and their guests can hardly hear themselves speak.

Lack of training in this area is not fair to the children, for they cannot know how to behave unless their parents teach them. "A well-ordered Christian household is a powerful argument in favor of the reality of the Christian religion." —*Patriarchs and Prophets*, p. 144.

"Let not a mother allow her mind to be occupied with too many things. . . . With the greatest diligence and the closest watchfulness she must care for the little ones who, if allowed, will follow every impulse springing out of the fullness of their unpracticed, ignorant hearts. In their exuberance of spirit they will give utterance to noise and turbulence in the home. This should be checked. Children will be just as happy if they are educated not to do these things. They are to be taught that when visitors come, they are to be quiet and respectful." —*Child Guidance*, p. 97.

Audrey Evans walked over to see her neighbor one

afternoon. Just as she came into the yard she noticed that her neighbor was coming out her own front door, followed by her two small children.

"Oh, I'm sorry," said Mrs. Evans. "I just ran over for a few minutes. I'll come back later, if that will be more convenient."

"I was just going for some peaches," answered Vera Smith. "I tried to get my mother to come and watch the children, but she's sick."

"I'll be glad to stay with your children," said Audrey Evans. "That is, if you won't be gone too long. I have to be home at 3:00."

"I'll be home long before that," Vera replied, "and I do thank you. I was going to take them, but it's always harder."

The 5-year-old boy was standing there scowling. "I hate you!" he said angrily. "I want to go." Audrey was not sure whom he was addressing, her or his mother.

"You can't go today, dear," his mother said. "You help Mrs. Evans with your little sister, and I'll bring you something from the store."

"You'd better!" the child replied rudely. Vera Smith looked at her friend with embarrassment, but said not a word of reproof to her ill-behaved child.

As soon as his mother drove away, the little boy came and stood in front of Mrs. Evans, feet planted wide; hands on his hips.

"I'm not going to obey one word you say," he said boldly, miniature chin raised in a gesture of pure defiance.

"Is that so?" replied Audrey. "Well, then, I guess I won't do what I had intended to do."

The child stood and regarded her a moment, a puzzled frown replacing his impudent glare.

"What were you goin' to do?" he asked, curiosity getting the better of him.

"Well, first, I thought I would take you and your little sister for a walk, and we could play in the sand by the river. Then I was going to put your little sister down for her nap and tell you some stories and draw some pictures for you.

But I don't like to hear people talk the way you talk when I come to visit. I'll have to wait till the next time I come, and see whether you are behaving any differently. Then we will see."

The child stood still for a moment and looked long at the visitor, his small faced filled with puzzlement. He had not met with this kind of talk before. Just what was going on here, anyway? He had a distinct sense of loss of some kind. Then he turned away with a very sad look pulling down the corners of his mouth. Rude children are not happy.

When the mother returned, the child asked her abruptly, right in front of the guest, "Mama, can Mrs. Evans tell stories?"

"I should say she can," said the mother. "You ought to hear her tell stories."

The child turned again and gazed at the guest with the same bewildered look. "Would you tell me stories next time you come—if I treat you nicely?" he asked in a subdued voice. Audrey Evans knelt down and put her arms around the little fellow. "Of course I will," she answered. "I love to tell stories to polite little boys."

The mother looked a little puzzled, but the child and Mrs. Evans understood each other perfectly. He wished that he had been kind to this most unusual lady. But he had never been shown how to treat guests in his home. Small as he was, he was aware that he had lost something. A seed was planted, however, and the next time Mrs. Evans visited, he got his story.

Training Necessary

All children, at times, do things that parents regret, but rudeness to guests will not often occur if the children have been reared to be respectful to their parents. This lesson is taught largely by example. Parents should take care to show respect for each other in front of their children. Children, also, are entitled to respect, and will respond by showing respect for others.

It takes much thought and attention to train a child to have the grace of politeness and respect toward visitors in the home, but the effort is worth while. "A child's truest graces consist in modesty and obedience—in attentive ears to hear the words of direction, in willing feet and hands to walk and work in the path of duty. And a child's true goodness will bring its own reward, even in this life."—*Ibid.*, p. 145.

For Further Reading . . .

Adams, Caren and Jennifer Fay.—**No More Secrets.** San Luis Obispo, Calif.: Impact Publishers, 1981. 90 pp.

A very helpful book to raise parents' awareness of facts surrounding the sexual assault of children. In addition, the authors provide concrete suggestions for talking to your child in advance, for prevention, and for what to do if your child has been assaulted. Although we could wish this might not be necessary, it is must reading for parents and other professionals dealing closely with children.

Ashton, Leila. **Today Is Friday.** Hagerstown, Md.: Review and Herald Publishing Association, 1978. 32 pp.

One of the My Church Teaches series for reading to the preschooler or to be read by lower grade children themselves. Leila Ashton, writer and illustrator, covers Friday activities—tidying, dusting, taking out trash, watering plants, cleaning, preparation of Sabbath dinner, baths, sunset worship, and tucking into bed—all presented in a happy context.

Barnes, Robert G., Jr. **Who's in Charge Here? Overcoming Power Struggles With Your Kids.** Waco, Tex.: Word Publishing Co., 1990.

This parenting primer covers such topics as parental responsibility and organization, spanking, the effects of day care and school, discipline, and building maturity. It emphasizes establishing an organized, consistent, and loving home environment grounded on scriptural principles.

Buntain, Ruth Jaeger. **Kids: How You Shape Their Lives.** Hagerstown, Md.: Review and Herald Publishing Association, 1991. 78 pp.

Drawing from 27 years' experience as a teacher, the author gives practical counsel on child rearing, with emphasis on imparting emotional and spiritual strength to the child.

Campbell, Ross. **How to Really Love Your Child.** Wheaton, Ill.: Victor Books, 1977. 132 pp.

Written by a psychiatrist, a very practical book on helping

the parent express love so the child can feel and understand it. Areas included are physical touch, positive eye contact, and focused attention.

Cline, Foster, and Jim Fay. **Parenting With Love and Logic: Teaching Children Responsibility.** Colorado Springs, Colo.: NavPress, 1990.

Teaches parents how to love in a healthy way, in turn helping children to learn responsibility and solve their own problems.

Curran, Dolores. **Stress and the Healthy Family.** Minneapolis: Harper and Row, 1987. 234 pp.

This is a very informative book that looks at how healthy families view their stresses and shows how they use their strengths to deal with them effectively during the various stages of family life. Not so much a "how to" book as a "how they" book, it provides a peek into others' family lives and practical help when everyday stresses test one's own family fabric.

Davis, Susan. **Never Again.** Hagerstown, Md.: Review and Herald Publishing Association, 1982. 32 pp.

The subject of death is often avoided or embroidered with fanciful tales. But children will believe and receive comfort from truth. This book is not only about death but also about grief. For grief brings healing and growth, and it is important that grief be allowed to do its work. In this story the child, Jeffie, passes through the grief stages of shock, anger, depression, understanding, and healing.

Dobson, James. **Dare to Discipline.** Wheaton, Ill.: Tyndale House, 1973. 198 pp.

Written from a wide background of teaching and counseling, the author includes material on respect and responsibility to children, discipline in the classroom, learning barriers, morality, and discipline.

————. **Hide or Seek.** Old Tappan, N.J.: Fleming H. Revell Co., 1974. 192 pp.

The author, in a very easily understood style, presents 10 ways in which parents and teachers can cultivate self-esteem in the child. Areas included are developing self-respect in the child, shaping the will without breaking the spirit, tools for building self-esteem, avoiding overprotection and dependency, maximizing educational potential, and preparation for adolescence.

______. **The Strong-willed Child.** Wheaton, Ill.: Tyndale House, 1978. 240 pp.

James Dobson in his inimitable way deals with the child whose will is oftentimes stronger than the parents'. The author is concerned with how to shape the will without breaking the spirit—a difficult but necessary accomplishment.

Dudley, Roger. **Passing on the Torch.** Hagerstown, Md.: Review and Herald Publishing Association, 1986. 191 pp.

The author draws on his experience as counselor and researcher to discuss religious values and how to make the work of parents in transmitting them to their children more effective.

______. **Why Teenagers Reject Religion—And What to Do About It.** Hagerstown, Md.: Review and Herald Publishing Association, 1978. 160 pp.

From a background of 10 years in youth ministry, Roger Dudley presents a careful study of the basic causes of youth alienation. In a scientific manner, the author explores the thinking and attitudes of academy-age young people and outlines plans and techniques that will reduce the alienation problem. The goal of this Christ-centered book is to unite youth and their parents and teachers in joyful fellowship with Jesus.

Elkind, David. **The Hurried Child.** Reading, Mass.: Addison-Wesley Publishing Co., 1981. 210 pp.

An excellent book for parents, teachers, and youth leaders that takes a hard look at children and stress. Psychologist David Elkind explores the unique burdens we place upon our children by expecting them, even pressuring them, to achieve and to grow up too fast, and offers insights, advice, and hope for solving these problems.

Flowers, Ronald M., Karen Flowers, and Betty Holbrook. **Caring**

for Families Today. 1990. Available from Department of Church Ministries, General Conference of Seventh-day Adventists, 12501 Old Columbia Pike, Silver Spring, Md. 20904. 85 pp.

A general guide for ministry to families in the local church. Includes a biblical rationale for family ministries, duties of the family ministries leader and committee, an outline of the special needs of families, and ideas for shaping, organizing, and implementing successful family ministries.

Garborg, Rolf. **The Family Blessing.** Waco, Tex.: Word Publishing Co., 1990.

This book describes how parents can impart a family blessing, a simple parental act that will help their children feel loved and cherished.

Ginott, Haim G. **Between Parent and Child.** New York: Macmillan Publishing Co., 1976. 256 pp.

The author's purpose is to show how the relationship between parent and child can be "less irritating and more rewarding," by dealing with specific solutions to daily situations. Areas covered include discipline, sex education, children's fears.

Holloway, Cheryl Woolsey. **Time Out for Moms.** Hagerstown, Md.: Review and Herald Publishing Association, 1991. 96 pp.

The author writes a delightful book for young mothers that bubbles over with honesty, warmth, and sparkling humor. In her short devotionals she shares moments from her family life that resulted in self-discovery, growth, adjustment, intense love, and turmoil. As you read, you'll find encouragement and strength for the demands of the day and enjoy the rare luxury of being nurtured.

Johnson, Jeannette. **Survival Tips for a Single Parent.** Hagerstown, Md.: Review and Herald Publishing Association, 1988. 32 pp.

The author shows you how to find time for laughter, love, and sharing. She outlines simple ideas for relieving tensions between you and your kids, and shows how children can help meet family challenges.

Joy, Donald M. **Bonding: Relationships in the Image of God.** Waco, Tex.: Word Books, 1985. 199 pp.

The basic thesis of this book is that "God's relationship with humans is one of intimate bonding, and all human intimacies are 'rehearsals' for the ultimate reunion of humans with their Creator." This is a book about why people need people and how the drama of human bonding has unfolded from birth to death in every family and every culture since Eden.

Kuzma, Kay. **Building Your Child's Character From the Inside Out.** Elgin, Ill.: David C. Cook Publishing Co., 1988. 266 pp. Available from Family Matters, P.O. Box 7000, Cleveland, Tenn. 37320.

This is an exciting journey that leads parents into discovering how to nurture and mold their children's character with sound spiritual values, and how to implement a tried-and-true character-building plan—a plan for building Christian character traits inside your children's hearts. The overall plan has been specially designed to be easily adapted to any child's age or interest level.

______. **The Day-Care Puzzle.** Boise, Idaho: Pacific Press Publishing Association, 1987. 30 pp. Available from Family Matters, P.O. Box 7000, Cleveland, Tenn. 37320.

Finding adequate child care is one of the most difficult problems for working parents. Most parents want someone who will train their children as well as keep them safe. And they want that person's values to approximate their own.

Kay Kuzma suggests ways to find the right kind of care for your child and how to maintain an ongoing evaluation of that care. She also suggests ways that you can help your child adjust to child care and how you can be a good day-care parent.

______. **Developing Your Child's Self-Worth.** Boise, Idaho: Pacific Press Publishing Association, 1989. 30 pp. Available from Family Matters, P.O. Box 7000, Cleveland, Tenn. 37320.

Dr. Kuzma outlines the basic elements of developing self-esteem in your young, impressionable children. She explains the symptoms of low self-esteem in children. She also points out typical parental behavior that can destroy a child's self-esteem and suggests alternatives.

______. **Filling Your Love Cup.** Redlands, California: Parent Scene, 1982. 84 pp. Family Matters, P.O. Box 7000, Cleveland, Tenn. 37320.

In this book you will learn how love creates love, how to discipline with love, how to cope and remain "cool," and how obnoxious people become lovable.

______. **Helping Kids Deal With Death.** Boise, Idaho: Pacific Press Publishing Association, 1987. 30 pp. Available from Family Matters, P.O. Box 7000, Cleveland, Tenn. 37320.

Kay Kuzma says, "Children often have profound questions about death, and they need the right answers." She points out that wrong answers about death can create fears in children's minds that may take years to erase. She also advises talking to children about death before someone close to them passes away—before it's even expected—so they are better able to cope when it suddenly happens. You will find her suggestions to be both practical and biblical. This book should be "must" reading for parents, teachers, and all others who have close relationships with children.

______. **Living With God's Kids.** Redlands, Calif.: Parent Scene, 1983. 141 pp. Available from Family Matters, P.O. Box 7000, Cleveland, Tenn. 37320, US$6; Cdn$7.50.

Kay Kuzma takes biblical principles and applies them to life today. She speaks directly to such current issues as how to build character in an imperfect world, finding time to parent in a whirlwind society, how to help children love and respect authority, helping children reach their potential, and teaching children to talk to God.

______. **Prime-Time Parenting.** New York: Rawson, Wade Publishers, Inc., 1980. 267 pp. Available from Family Matters, P.O. Box 7000, Cleveland, Tenn. 37320.

If you worry that your pressured, hectic life is depriving your children, this book will show you how to get the biggest benefits from the time you do have together. You can, says author Kay Kuzma, combine your own concerns and career with the job of parenting, and raise happy, healthy children.

Prime-Time Parenting is the complete guide for working parents, single parents, and busy homemakers.

______. **To Understand Your Child.** Redlands, Calif.: Parent Scene, 1985. 131 pp. Family Matters, P.O. Box 7000, Cleveland, Tenn. 37320.

This is a practical "how to" guide for parents of young children, offering specific strategies to meet a child's need for love and trust, promote healthy attitudes and behavior, handle explosive emotions, develop self-control and responsibility, and build enduring self-worth.

______. **Working Mothers.** Los Angeles: Stratford Press. 1981. 269 pp. Available from Family Matters, P.O. Box 7000, Cleveland, Tenn. 37320.

Working Mothers is a comprehensive sourcebook for all busy mothers, teaching how to get the biggest benefits from the limited time you have to spend with your children. It offers practical solutions to such problems as finding competent child care, guilt, fatigue, and job/family conflicts. It shows you how to fulfill personal and family needs, how to help your children become self-disciplined, and how to shape your family into a strong, mutually supportive team.

Lantry, Eileen. **Family Guide to Sabbath Nature Activities.** Boise, Idaho: Pacific Press Publishing Association, 1980. 127 pp.

The book has been planned as a guide to help parents develop in their children a love for God and nature, and a means whereby parents and children can share in the joys of true Sabbathkeeping. The ideas proposed have been tried by the author, who is a mother herself, and can be easily adapted to fit other environments. Based on Ellen G. White counsel, the book can help make the Sabbath a delight to the family.

MacDonald, Gordon. **The Effective Father.** Wheaton, Ill.: Tyndale House Publishers, Inc., 1977. 256 pp.

Based on his Bible study, his pastoral counseling experiences and his own family life, the author offers an inspiring and insightful, yet practical, and interesting guide to fathering.

Meier, Paul, and Richard Meier. **Family Foundations.** Grand Rapids: Baker Book House, 1981. 96 pp.

A good general volume on many questions that come up while rearing a family in today's world. No pat solutions, but definitely encouragement, humor, and a deep Christian basis for all family successes. Chapter titles are: "A Spiritual Base," "Genuine Love," "Gut-Level Communication," "Discipline," "Consistency," "Setting the Example," and "Proper Leadership Roles."

Robinson, Glen. **Fifty-two Things to Do on Sabbath.** Hagerstown, Md.: Review and Herald Publishing Association, 1983, 32 pp.

A book of practical suggestions for Sabbath activities that will involve both the adult and the child.

Schock, Bernie A. **Remodeling the Family: A Radical Plan for Restoring the Home.** Brentwood, Tenn.: Wolgemuth and Hyatt, 1990.

Many of our parents grew up in families that, though financially poor, were emotionally and relationally rich beyond measure. According to the author, parents and families should not count on our culture to provide entertainment, instruction, and guidance, and have lost the meaning of home. While not advocating a return to the past, he does challenge parents to reassert their role in their children's educational, vocational, spiritual, social, and physical development.

Smedes, Lewis B. **Caring and Commitment: Learning to Live the Love We Promise.** San Francisco: Harper and Row, 1988. 153 pp.

This book examines the meaning of commitment in friendship, in marriage, in relationships between parents and their children. It includes a section on crises in relationships, including conflict of culture, religious faith, needs, and conscience. How to bring forgiveness, healing, and renewal to broken commitments is a part of the book that is especially valuable.

Smith, Virginia Watts. **The Single Parent.** Old Tappan, N.J.: Fleming H. Revell Co., 1983. 192 pp.

Drawn from her own struggles, the author has written a book of very practical suggestions, filled with Christian hope, for the single parent. Areas that she has included are emotions, sexual adjustment, parental behavior problems, society and the single, and emotionally damaged children.

Spruill, Karen. **The Making of a Mother.** Hagerstown, Md.: Review and Herald Publishing Association, 1988. 128 pp.

In this personal and surprisingly honest book, the author shares the discoveries that set her free from feelings of loneliness, frustration, and inadequacy. She also offers practical advice on breast-feeding, toilet training, money matters, self-forgiveness, and discipline.

Van Pelt, Nancy L. **The Compleat Parent.** Hagerstown, Md.: Review and Herald Publishing Association, 1985. 224 pp.

Written by a mother of three and teacher of elementary and high school students, this is a book of easy-to-learn, easy-to-use ways of effective disciplining. Areas include child's self-respect, communication, character development, nutrition, sex education, sibling rivalry, drug prevention, and roles of parents.

______. **The Compleat Parent Workbook.** Hagerstown, Md.: Review and Herald Publishing Association, 1985. 76 pp.

This workbook provides ways for parents to evaluate themselves and their relationships with their children.

White, Ellen G. **Child Guidance.** Hagerstown, Md.: Review and Herald Publishing Association, 1954. 616 pp. US$11.95; Cdn$14.95.

In numerous books but more particularly in her articles on practical Christian living that appeared in various journals, Mrs. White sets forth a wealth of counsel to parents. Only the thoughtful and prayerful perusal of the significant counsels of this volume can reveal the tremendous and far-reaching influence of training the child properly as God has placed the responsibility with parents.

______. **Counsels to Parents, Teachers, and Students.** Boise, Idaho: Pacific Press Publishing Association, 1913, 1943. 575 pp.

Counsel is given on conducting a school, with special attention on subject matter, discipline, and objectives to be emphasized.

_____. **Fundamentals of Christian Education.** Hagerstown, Md.: Review and Herald Publishing Association, 1923. 576 pp.

A reprinting of Ellen G. White articles having a bearing on the subject of education, as published in the journals of the church, out-of-print Christian Temperance and Bible Hygiene (1890), and Special Testimonies on Education (cir. 1897).

_____. **Happiness Homemade.** Hagerstown, Md.: Review and Herald Publishing Association, 1971. 188 pp. (Study guide also available.)

Materials compiled from the writings of Ellen G. White covering all areas of family life, such as building and furnishing the home, fathers, mothers, the unborn child, finance, and recreation.

Josephine Cunnington Edwards Collector's Set

Johnnie, Come Home
Meet Johnnie, a country-bred misfit who is rarely out of trouble, often on the road, and who can never manage to shoot the right thing when he shoulders a gun! This lively story traces the boyish adventures that lead to Johnnie's dedication to the mission field. Formerly entitled *And I John Saw.*

The Enchanted Pillowcase and Other Stories
The story of Alice Princess, a beautiful orphaned child who is rescued from hateful, greedy relatives and led to the Lord through a series of astonishing events. Two additional stories add to your reading pleasure.

Reuben's Portion
This best-seller tells the story of an aristocrat who loses everything in the Civil War but his pride. He determines to build a new dynasty, but he is rejecting the only foundation that can bear the weight of his dream.

Faded Love
Love brought this man and woman together. Then success drove them apart. This family saga spans three generations. Formerly entitled *Unto a Knowledge of the Truth.*

Paper, US$7.95, Cdn$9.95 each.
US$29.95, Cdn$37.45, set.

Practical Help and Spiritual Strength for Young Mothers

Time Out for Moms
Cheryl Woolsey Holloway's delightful devotional book for young mothers bubbles over with warmth and sparkling humor. She shares moments drawn from her family life that have resulted in self-discovery, growth, adjustment, intense love, and turmoil. Mothers will find encouragement and strength and enjoy the rare luxury of being nurtured. Paper, 94 pages. US$6.95, Cdn$8.70.

Help! I'm a Mother!
Drawing from years of experience as a mother and OB nurse, Nancy Beck Irland offers sensitive advice on how to cope with motherhood. Emotional adjustment for mom, a baby's different cries, what to do when the baby is sick, adjusting to the second and third baby—and much more—are covered in this practical book. Paper, 96 pages. US$6.95, Cdn$8.70.

The Making of a Mother
Karen Spruill writes a surprisingly frank and personal book about motherhood. She shares her secret battles with frustration and feelings of inadequacy. Then she tells what it took to set her free. She also gives tried-and-true advice on breast feeding, toilet training, self-forgiveness, and money matters. "The chapter on discipline alone is worth the price of the book," says fellow author and mother June Strong. Paper, 128 pages. US$7.95, Cdn$9.95.

Helpful Books for Parents and Teachers

Passing On the Torch
This best-seller by Roger Dudley shows parents and teachers how they can successfully pass their spiritual values on to children and teens. Paper, 192 pages. US$2.95, Cdn$3.70.

The World of the Adventist Teenager
Discover what teens *really* think about their parents, schools, and church standards. Roger Dudley and Janet Leigh Kangas provide eye-opening information about teen attitudes and behavior and offer practical suggestions for a new emphasis in teen ministry. Paper, 141 pages. US$11.95, Cdn$14.95.

Kids: How You Shape Their Lives
Drawing from 27 years' experience as a teacher, Ruth Buntain gives practical counsel on child rearing, with emphasis on imparting emotional and spiritual strength to the child. Paper, 78 pages. US$6.50, Cdn$8.10.

It Shouldn't Hurt to Be a Child
What child abuse is, how to detect it, what to do about it, and how to prevent it are the topics covered in this little booklet by Dianne Vasi. There is also a list of professional agencies to contact for help. Paper, 32 pages. US$.79, Cdn$1.00.

To order, call **1-800-765-6955** or write to ABC Mailing Service, P.O. Box 1119, Hagerstown, MD 21741. Send check or money order. Enclose applicable sales tax and 15 percent (minimum US$2.50) for postage and handling. Prices and availability subject to change without notice. Add 7 percent GST in Canada.